Contemporary Silver

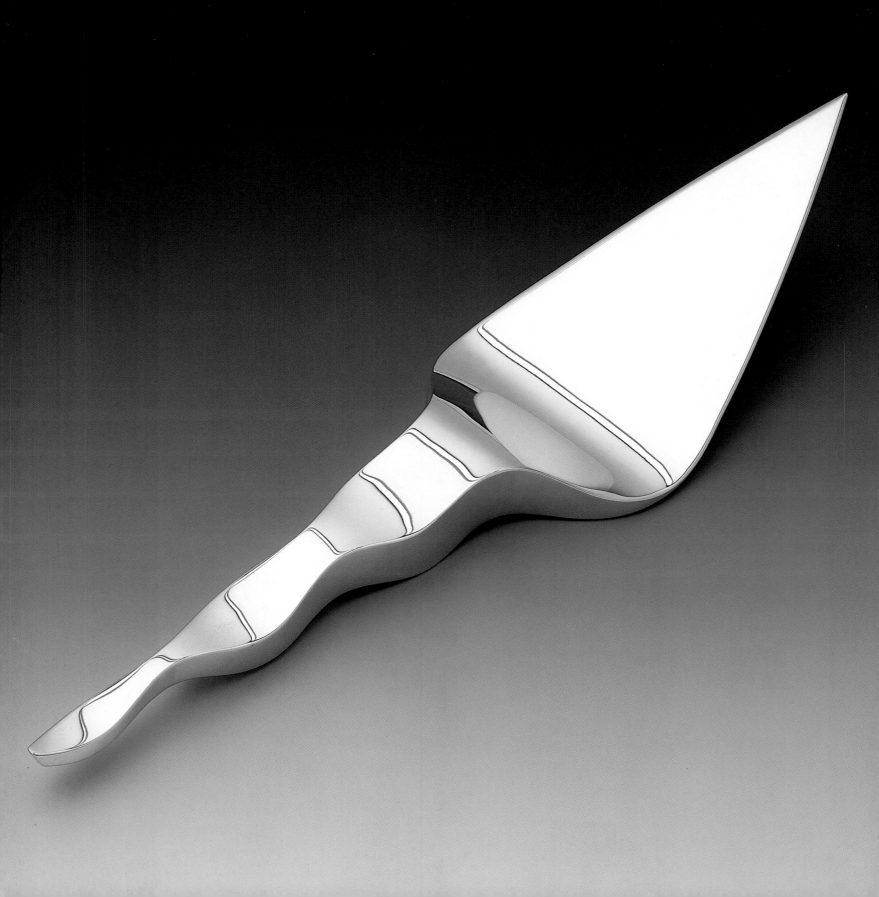

Contemporary Silver

commissioning

designing

collecting

Benton Seymour Rabinovitch

Helen Clifford

MERRELL

To Flora and Alan

Cover: David Peterson (see pp. 138–39)
Page 2: Toby Russell (see pp. 82–83)
Page 3, top: Andrea Schweitzer (pp. 142–43)
Page 3, bottom: Anthony Elson (pp. 46–47)
Pages 4–5: Jane Short (detail; see pp. 84–85)
Pages 6–7: Suzanne Amendolara (detail; see pp. 96–97)
Page 8: Wally Gilbert (detail; see pp. 48–49)
Page 23: Komelia Hongja Okim (detail; see pp. 134–35)
Page 25: Jacqueline Mina (detail; see pp. 74–75)
Pages 26–27: Michael Lloyd (detail; see pp. 64–65)

First published 2000 by
Merrell Publishers Limited

Text © 2000 Benton Seymour Rabinovitch and Helen Clifford
Foreword © 2000 Rosemary Ransome Wallis/Worshipful Company of Goldsmiths
Photographs © 2000 Benton Seymour Rabinovitch

British Library Cataloguing-in-Publication Data
Rabinovitch, B. Seymour
Contemporary silver : commissioning, designing, collecting
1.Silverwork 2.Silverwork – Design 3.Silverwork – History
4.Silverwork – Collectors and collecting
I.Title II.Clifford, Helen
739.2'3

ISBN 1 85894 104 0

Distributed in the USA and Canada by Rizzoli International Publishers, Inc.
through St Martin's Press, 175 Fifth Avenue, New York, New York 10010

Edited by Iain Ross and Vanessa Brett. Designed by Maggi Smith

Produced by Merrell Publishers Limited
42 Southwark Street
London SE1 1UN
www.merrellpublishers.com

Printed and bound in Italy

Contents

Acknowledgements   6

Foreword by Rosemary Ransome Wallis   7

1   Introduction   9

2   **Patronage**
     How to commission silver today   10

3   **Historical Background**
     Servers in the eighteenth and nineteenth centuries   15

4   **Silver Design in Britain and America**
     1950–2000   18

5   **Looking at the Collection**   24

6   **The Collection**   26
     British Silversmiths   28
     American Silversmiths   97

7   **Information**
     Notes   154
     Glossary   156
     Further Reading   158
     Useful Addresses   158
     Index   159

Acknowledgements

The authors offer their deepest thanks to Vanessa Brett for her crucial early encouragement and for volunteering to undertake a burdensome initial editorial role that was instrumental in shaping this project and propelling it towards publication.

We are grateful to Rosemary Ransome Wallis, Curator of the Worshipful Company of Goldsmiths, for writing the Foreword, for her guidance in craft matters, and for her advice in the selection of a number of the British silversmiths. Others at Goldsmiths' Hall, David Beasley, Lesley Leader and Victoria Lane, also have our gratitude for their unstinting assistance.

We thank all the silversmiths who have had a part in this project – for the pleasure of the associations, for many special acts of co-operation and for the lasting enjoyment and enlightenment their efforts have provided. We appreciate early advice from John Marshall and Roger Horner.

Many individuals assisted in smaller or larger measure, explicitly or implicitly, in our task and we value their help. They include Philippa Glanville (now Director at Waddesdon Manor), Richard Edgecumbe and Eric Turner of the Metalwork Department of the Victoria and Albert Museum, for sharing their expertise; Tony Ford and Andrew Ryan of the Crafts Council in London for helpful encouragement and assessment; and Michael Rowe of the Royal College of Art for kindly providing the statistics on graduation from the Department of Silversmithing, Metalwork and Jewellery. Gareth Harris and Dennis Smith explained many technical points from their workshop at Hatton Garden, London. We would also like to acknowledge the inspiration found in the manifold patronage of the P&O Makower Trust, Oxfordshire.

Fervent thanks to BSR's capable and tolerant secretary Katharine Smith, and her gracious and efficient alternate, Karen Fincher. We also thank photographers Marsha and Michael Burns for their fine work.

We appreciate the outstanding co-operation we have received from Merrell Publishers, in particular from Julian Honer, Iain Ross, Matt Hervey, Kate Ward and Jennifer Wright. We would also like to thank designer Maggi Smith for her tremendous work on this book.

Foreword

In 1995, the exhibition *Slices of Silver* at Goldsmiths' Hall introduced the Company and the public to a mesmeric collection of forty-two silver fish servers and cake slices by contemporary British and American silversmiths.

This collection, which has grown in number since then, has a unique and special quality. It is proof of the skill and diversity of contemporary silversmiths. Each artist-craftsman has responded to the familiar form of the server in an individual way, combining function and decoration in an astonishingly diverse range of interpretations. Each piece becomes an enchanting, decorative work of art. This human quality has been achieved through the patronage of Professor Rabinovitch, who establishes a charming rapport with each artist, always requesting them to be unfettered creatively. The reaction of modern silversmiths is not only to be freely creative but also to honour their patron by giving him their best work.

This collection is testimony to the significant contribution that one individual can make to support the craft.

Rosemary Ransome Wallis
Curator, Worshipful Company of Goldsmiths

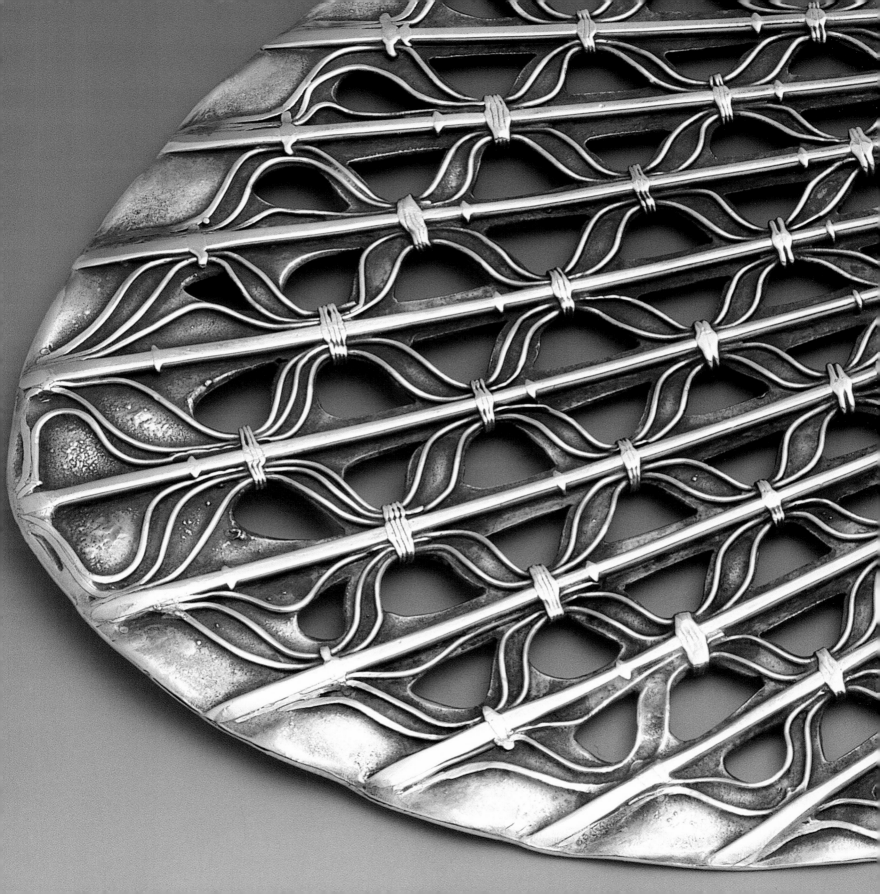

1 Introduction

This book is based on a collection of newly commissioned broad-bladed silver servers. They are also commonly called 'slices'. One need not be a 'collector' to have something specially made. Anyone can commission an object, in any material, for whatever reason. The article may be practical or merely decorative, pure self-indulgence or a gift.

The book actually has its origins in a collection of antique broad-bladed silver servers – such as fish and cake slices – of the eighteenth and nineteenth centuries.[1] As an outcome of that activity, the commissioning of what, at this time, comprises some sixty pieces, began towards the end of the 1980s and had two purposes: first, a modest effort to support independent silversmiths and their craft; secondly, to provide a comparative study of contemporary styles in metalsmithing relating to one type of object: the broad-bladed server.

The narrow focus of the present collection has the advantage of making easier the comparisons between the styles current among silversmiths and also makes possible a survey – a snapshot – of the techniques in vogue today. The silversmiths were given complete freedom to create an article of their own inspiration and design. Their challenge was to create and convey beauty through a vehicle, the slice, an implement that is ostensibly a utilitarian form. But if a question arose or was in doubt, it was always emphasized that it was deemed better to feed the spirit rather than the stomach, and that artistic and aesthetic considerations should take precedence over function. Because a comparable number of silversmiths from Britain and America were commissioned, the collection also reveals differences and similarities between these two cultures and shows the depth of cross-cultural influence.

But why the interest in broad-bladed servers in the first place, as in the original antique collection? Although servers are functional implements, they do lend themselves to adornment by piercing, chasing, engraving, enamelling and so on. The silversmiths represented here come from a wide range of backgrounds: trade and art-school trained jewellers, blacksmiths, sculptors, teachers, poets, and painters. Yet all have made the decision to work in silver. The philosophy and practice of these makers reflect their training, motivation, work situation and response to the artistic *Zeitgeist*, all of which help to determine the relative emphasis placed by them on various aspects of design and decoration. Each article is a unique configuration that sometimes results in the triumph of the sculptural and ornamental over the practical. Always there is the undercurrent of historical stylistic competition between naturalistic, biomorphic influences and more severe, geometric shapes. The result has been the creation of a panoply of beauty and excitement.

Many traditional crafts have languished in the face of competition from industrial manufacture. Hand-wrought silversmithing is one of many that have felt pressure from the mechanization and commercialization of manufacturing firms since the nineteenth century. This has made many people fear for the survival of the craft and its techniques, and concern has been manifest for a long time. Indeed, as the twentieth century drew to a close, a new 'threat' from computer control of fabrication was a focus of debate: will craftsmen and craftswomen become obsolete?[2] From early in the century leading silversmiths, such as Omar Ramsden, keenly felt the need for the support of individual silversmiths and encouraged direct commissioning.[3] The Worshipful Company of Goldsmiths, which oversees the craft in England, is a powerful force in support of the craft and craftsmanship as well as the trade.

One of the purposes of this volume is to encourage the commissioning of silver articles and to explain how to go about it. Of course, much of the exposition applies to any craft interest. The whys and hows of this pursuit are discussed in an effort to encourage private individuals to commission. For at the present time silversmiths receive orders mainly from institutions and corporations, although some individuals do commission a whole range of objects. In 1996, for example, the Goldsmiths' Company exhibited dozens of newly commissioned napkin rings. These 'humble' objects did not fail to provide an impressive display of beauty and novelty. Personal commissioning is a positive influence on the promotion and preservation of the craft and needs to become more widespread.

Collectors – those who regularly acquire objects that are not necessities – are considered by some to be a strange breed who may, at times, find great difficulty in justifying their compulsive behaviour. We dismiss any who count monetary gain as the incentive for their obsessive zeal. Some collectors gather the objects of their affection and merely delight in the quantity of accumulated material. Most, however, seek broader intellectual reasons and provide a scholarly contribution, to a greater or lesser extent, to some facet of knowledge. Moreover, the collecting of objects often serves as an entrée to other areas of knowledge – political, historical or social – and also to the skills of the craft.

2 Patronage: how to commission silver today

It is useful to make a distinction between two types of private support of the arts. The first, and perhaps the most commonly understood today, is the enlightened, wealthy donor who contributes to the administration and collections of museums and institutes. In most cases, this results in the acquisition of works by artists long gone or, if of this century, who are no longer active. The second involves the direct support of an artist by commissioning work. Of course, the patron need not be an individual but, as is often the case today, a company, corporation, institution or other group. In the context of silver, the Worshipful Company of Goldsmiths in London is a notable example.

The key to artistic style and technique is confidence, and that is bred by patronage Graham Hughes

How does support of the arts affect society? At the very least, it fosters a more vibrant, intellectually and aesthetically stimulating environment: the difference between living in a desert or in a garden. Whether locally or country-wide, the difference is that between a dynamic, exciting and forward-looking society and one that tends to be inward-looking. The economic advantages that accrue to a progressive society that supports education and the arts are widely manifest in today's world.

Historically, the commissioning of silver has been subject, more than any other area of the arts, to pressures of politics, economics and taste, owing to its close ties to currency and resultant meltings. Its central role in church, state and the domestic life of the wealthy was maintained until the end of the nineteenth century. It is only in the last one hundred years that tremendous social changes, combined with new manufacturing techniques and new materials (notably plastics and stainless steel), have caused confusion in the silversmiths' trade and among its patrons. The Christian religion requires altar plate, and, particularly in traditionally Catholic countries, architects and patrons of churches and private chapels have used precious metals to enhance their earthly and spiritual aspirations. In government and in the high ranks of political families, silver was a necessary adjunct of power and status. Gifts between rulers and between monarchs and their courtiers (for example the English tradition of New Year gifts), while not exclusively the work of silversmiths, were at certain times a major part of their output. Success on the battlefield, in political alliances, in sporting prowess, in commerce and in arranged marriages and healthy childbirth were commemorated by commissioning of plate. These items were not, until the nineteenth century, usually 'bought off the shelf'; they were specially ordered, sometimes with great care and thought and sometimes at immense cost. Articles for use in the bedroom (showy toilet sets) and dining room (extensive dinner services and all the accoutrements that attended the increasing sophistication of eating habits) were, however, the principal areas for private patronage.

What I want is silver to become part of everyday life. I wish people ate their meals off silver and then bunged it in the dishwasher Justine Huntley

Networking by both patron and artist, word-of-mouth recommendation, family and business connections, competitive shopping, gambling on lotteries – familiar features of our lives today – all played their part in the commissioning of plate. Where we differ in attitude today is in a tendency to hold on to the past, perhaps encouraged by prices realized on the open market, and this has particularly affected the commissioning of new silver even at a time when the raw material is relatively cheap and no longer has any relationship with currency. No longer is worn-out, bad-quality, unfashionable or impractical silver melted, recycled and re-made on a regular basis. If silver is used in the home, it is all too often 'antique' rather than newly made. It is here that patronage of contemporary work needs the greatest encouragement.

The twentieth century has been an exciting period – more so, probably, than the nineteenth – and people should be aware that much wonderful and significant work is being wrought today. The opportunity to be part of this action is a very special boon. As Vanessa Brett has remarked, the pleasure we derive from viewing, holding or owning the products of past centuries should prompt us to leave behind objects from our own time, for the enjoyment and edification of future generations.[1] Thus anyone can be the agent of the creation of articles of beauty and significance that are part of the story of our culture and civilization, a story that will be read by later generations, who will then share our enjoyment of these objects.

The Silversmith

This book, and the collection on which it is based, is concerned with the work of men and women who are generally described as 'artist silversmiths'. For the most part they have their own workshop and may, or may not, employ assistants or work in a partnership. Sometimes they have part of a job done by specialists – for example spinning or engraving, particularly if the job develops into a short 'run' rather than a 'one-off' – but they are responsible for the design and manufacture of any object. Many work from home. Their products are hand-wrought.

It gives me the greatest satisfaction to know that the customer has been at least partially involved in the aesthetic result Michael Brophy

Of course, those who work for the large manufacturing companies are also very skilled. However, the products on which they work, usually to someone else's design and as employees, are of a different genre. Large retail outlets, such as Asprey & Garrard in the United Kingdom, Tiffany and Gorham in the United States or Bulgari, Cartier and Christofle on the Continent, have their own workshops in which they employ designers and craftsmen to do commissioned work and repairs and speculative pieces for sale in their shops. They also sometimes have 'commercial' pieces made for them by independent silversmiths, who are sometimes glad of the work if personal commissions are thin on the ground. These retailers also buy in silver from manufacturing firms for resale (for example Oneida, International Silver and many more), and these are very often reproduction wares or mass-production pieces catering for a buying public with a wide variety of tastes and sizes of pocket. Such pieces can also be bought by mail-order on the internet, or in department stores and jewellery shops in most cities. Much of this trade is in fact in electroplated wares. Increasingly, these goods are manufactured in the Far East. This market is not for personal commissioned work and is not what this book seeks to support. It is the difference between owning a painting by Rembrandt and a finely printed image of his work; both require skill, but only one is art. Having said that, in an age when silver struggles to maintain its market at all, because fashion has shifted to plastics and stainless steel, the purchase of any good-quality silver supports the trade and thus promotes this wonderful material.

The irony is that, given the current state of things, small craft businesses are the future of industry Brian Asquith

Some silversmiths have established their own shops and deal with the public in the same manner, but on a smaller scale, as the large firms just mentioned. They may also depend on commissioned work. Many sell through galleries, fairs, exhibitions and the like. In this way they hope that their work will find wider recognition, or at least that they may smooth out the economic bumps of dependence on commissioned work. Recently, both Asprey and Garrard (now consolidated as Asprey & Garrard) in London have held selling exhibitions that included the work of several silversmiths who feature in this book, thus attempting to introduce their clients to this different approach to the metal. Some of the more successful, and perhaps more fortunate, artists find part-time or full-time employment on the faculties of educational institutions. In general, professional craftsmen and crafts-women share a problem with other artists, musicians, actors, entertainers and so on, many of whom depend on part-time work outside their major field for their subsistence.

The Patron

Patronage comes from all sectors of society. Churches commission crosses, candelabra, chalices, alms plates, pyxes and a variety of other articles. In the United Kingdom, the Lichfield Cathedral commission of 1991, of some nineteen silversmiths, was a notable event of recent times. So also has been the creation of The Silver Trust, one of the initial purposes of which was to endow the residence of the Prime Minister at 10 Downing Street with hand-wrought contemporary silver. In the United States, the White House has sought embellishment by contributions from a large number of craftsmen. Clubs of all sorts, trophy donors, regimental and military units, corporations, associations, governmental agencies, civic bodies and the like constitute part of a long list of patrons. Thus in 1993, Sheffield City Council initiated the commission of a canteen of cutlery from thirty-seven silversmiths to commemorate seven hundred years of the cutlery trade and as a celebration of the millennium. But an increasingly necessary component of such sponsorship is the individual – necessary for the survival of the silversmiths, desirable for the welfare of the craft.

When you told me to make the server as if it would be my own … that insight into an artist's mind is very rare … was very significant for me

Harold Schremmer

In a more personal vein, one of the bonuses of the present collection has been the opportunity to meet many of the silversmiths, to see their work places and even to form friendships. This is easier in the United Kingdom since London is such an important centre of work and focus of travel. By contrast, the United States is so large and so diverse in its artistic centres that much of the interaction was carried on by letter and by telephone: the latter particularly useful for providing a personal touch.

Doing It!

Most silver purchases by the general public today are for objects such as picture frames, flatware, tea and coffee pots and related equipment of the dining and tea table. These purchases are likely to be made at commercial silver shops and stores that handle the wares of the big commercial manufacturers such as Oneida, International Silver, Towle, Gorham, Vander, Rogers, Hutton and other sources. As a starter, commissioning is more likely to refer to gift or celebratory items, whether christenings – the celebrated silver spoon in the mouth – birthdays, anniversaries, weddings, retirements or the like.

A prospective patron might easily be intimidated by the apparent impenetrability of the system of direct commissioning. How does one go about it? Fairly easily, with just a little initial effort! Like many other activities, one gains increasing comfort and ease with practice. The process of undertaking to commission a piece of silver can be broken down into stages: choosing a maker; cost; design; and liaising with the craftsman.

Choosing a Maker

This book provides a start in understanding the style in which a selected group of artists work. Books and catalogues that may be useful and illustrate the work of contemporary silversmiths, and places where you can see contemporary silver, are listed on page 158. If it is relatively easy for you to visit the workshop of a silversmith (commercial silverware vendors are here excluded), you may examine their work and their credentials (qualifications, prior commissions, awards etc.). But there are not many silversmiths who have such retail outlets and so one has to seek elsewhere. Many colleges and technical schools have fine metalworkers on their staff, as well as library resources. The information on page 158 will be of assistance. Recourse to the Web can also be helpful.

I take pride in the relationship between myself and the person commissioning the work and gain a great deal of satisfaction from it Rod Kelly

When you have made a short list of silversmiths – or have chosen one whose work looks appealing – a visit to a studio, a telephone call or a letter explaining your interest should lead to an exploratory exchange of information relating to feasibility, price, schedule and other arrangements – including the opportunity to withdraw. The person whose work is most pleasing to you, and with whom you will be able to do business, is the one to choose. But bear in mind the high degree of subjectivity involved; advice from any informed source may be very useful.

Design

The client first decides the type of object that is wanted: bowl, candlestick, cutlery and so on. One may then supply a rough drawing or other specification – preferably written rather than entirely oral – of the intended object. This may be purposely vague or very specific, to suit your needs. A drawing from the silversmith should then give expression to their design conception, embodying the intention of the client. The client can dictate the amount of freedom of expression that is allowed the craftsman, but the basic design should be fixed before one finally agrees to proceed with the project. This is

I hope my work reflects my deep love of nature. It is a celebration of our surroundings...

Michael Lloyd

certainly the case when a company, institution or regiment commissions a piece, the character of which is largely fixed by precedent, their logo, or in repairing or matching defective or missing parts of a set. One may relish the opportunity to exercise one's own talent at design, thus making the article a very personal one. On the other hand, an exchange of views with the artist can lead to a happy concordance. Alternatively, having chosen the silversmith because of a liking for previous examples of their work, one may simply leave the design in their hands. This last alternative was the case for the present collection, which constitutes a study of contemporary design. From the point of view of the artist, there is no doubt that a high degree of freedom of design is the happiest situation. However, most silversmiths understand, are responsive to the fact, and even expect, that some restrictive design criteria and features, including financial, will be required. The American smith William Frederick perceives such restrictions as a challenge that can prove to be a kind of bonus. Wally Gilbert has put the matter very cogently:

Any piece of work is a more or less successful partnership between the material and the *designer-maker* [our italics], through the medium of the process. A new element, in the form of the ideas of the patron, is brought into the equation, which can give new force and direction for development. There is always danger (for the craftsman) of stagnation through ... repetition of ideas when working in isolation, as many craftspeople do. A commission is therefore a three-way partnership.

A valuable advantage to the client in dealing directly with the silversmith is personal involvement. How else can one participate on such a level with a living artist? It can be illuminating and exciting – a window on, or a peek at, a new world for anyone who has not done this before. There is enormous pleasure in being part, great or small, of the creative process that goes into the making of an object – be it for oneself or a gift to another – which gives it a very personal significance. Indeed, the attachment to an intended gift may become so great that it never leaves your possession – or at the very least may necessitate a duplicate!

Cost

The relative cost of commissioning a piece as opposed to buying a new object off the shelf at some retail shop must first be considered. By and large, one may expect that a commissioned piece will cost no more, and perhaps less, than a similar object from a commercial supplier. Although frequenters of antique shops and stalls may do better monetarily than either of these alternatives, the advantage of buying something new lies probably with the silversmith. Of course, the size, complexity and importance of the piece also regulate the magnitude of the expenditure. A covered tankard is in a different price bracket to a child's cup; extensive engraving or other ornamentation will add to the outlay.

Rather than relying on the surface detail I feel that the form alone should provide both function and aesthetic   Toby Russell

What will commissioning cost? Depending on the nature of the item, this can be anything from tens of pounds (or dollars) to thousands. There is an equivalence of price in pounds and dollars: roughly speaking, a given article comes in at the same number in the United Kingdom as in the United States. The best approach is to say frankly what you can afford. Discussion with the silversmith will quickly reveal whether this is realistic for the end intended. In many instances the nature of the commission can be tailored to the patron's purse.

Consider that what you get is a one-of-a-kind piece, made just for you – not one of a hundred or a thousand like it. When the American craftsman John Marshall was asked to make eight cutlery place settings to his own design he balked even at that: "Too repetitive, a dull enterprise". "How about eight place settings, each to be a different design?" They were so made! But it is for you, the client, to decide whether you wish to be persuaded by the silversmith into something not originally intended.

It is a poor investment to skimp on the weight of a piece. The cost of materials is relatively much smaller than that of the labour, an inversion of relative values from earlier centuries when silver had the value of coinage and silversmiths were often also bankers. A substantial item asserts its presence: it demands regard. No matter how much time and effort the fabrication of a piece might take, a lightweight and flimsy 'feel' automatically undercuts its merit.

An important rule that should always be followed is never to undertake the commission of an object purely as a financial investment.

Schedule

Allow as much time as possible. There are many factors to take into consideration, such as how busy the silversmith is, and this may depend on luck: whether you get in just before some big project or have to wait on its completion. Depending on what you are asking to be made, and by whom, the interval between starting the whole project going and receiving the finished object can be from one month to two years.

If the object is to be given as a gift on an anniversary or retirement – if the date of presentation is fundamental to its purpose – you *must* think ahead and make this date clear to the silversmith from the outset.

Summary: A Step-by-Step Guide

- Decide what type of article you want and roughly how much you wish to spend.
- Have clearly in mind alternative possibilities relating to function, price, material and surface decoration. Will this object be used every day or will it be put on a shelf for decoration?
- Make a rough sketch of your intended object, or be able to refer to illustrations of a similar piece. Be absolutely clear about whether you want any personal logo, inscription, initials *etc.*
- Decide on a silversmith. For the most part silversmiths do not enter into competitive tendering for work, either in terms of design or price, against fellow silversmiths. If you like the kind of work they do, they will adapt design and cost until you reach an agreement.
- Have a personal chat if possible and then lay out in detail in a letter all your thoughts relating to price, type of article and personalized features. Make clear what reliance you are placing on the silversmith's design ability.
- Get in writing a schedule, estimated price, and a rough drawing, to include materials, of the object. This must be a record for both patron and silversmith. At this stage the silversmith may ask for a deposit, usually a percentage of the agreed final cost. If now, or at any time after this, you decide to withdraw from the project, you should be prepared to pay for the silversmith's time and costs in working on the designs.
- Agree to consult promptly on any questions that may arise. There should be a record (a drawing) of any design changes as they occur, and ultimately a finished drawing. Make sure you understand the dimensions correctly.
- Keep yourself informed on progress, but do not be a nag.
- Pay the bill promptly.

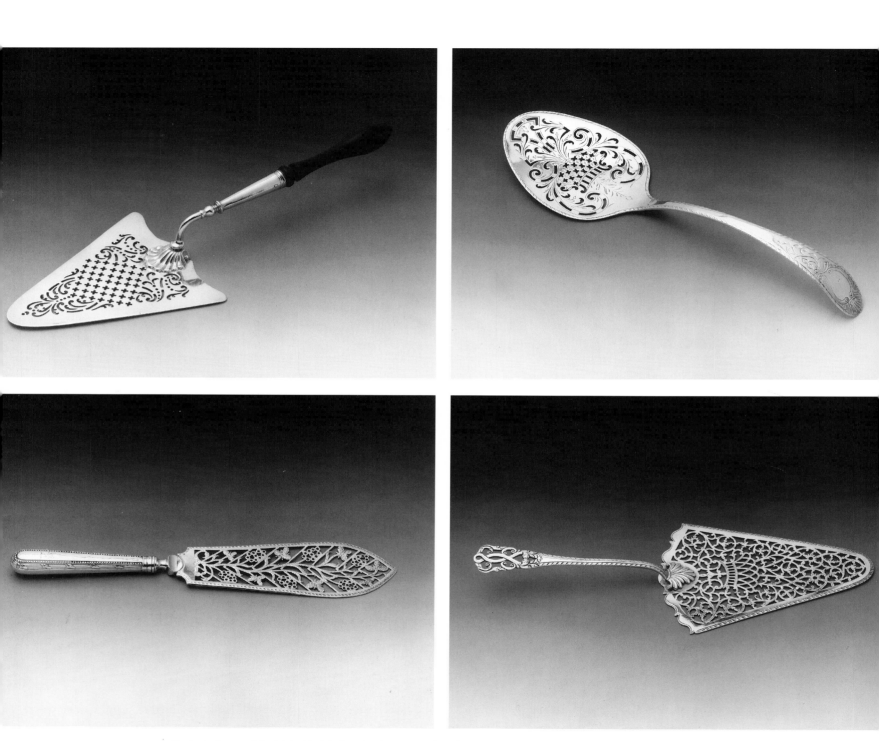

Clockwise from top left: **1** John Hugh le Sage, London 1746, 13¼ in. (33.5 cm); **2** Charles Townsend, Dublin 1773, 13¾ in. (35 cm)
3 Basile Denn, London 1775, 11⅔ in. (29.5 cm); **4** Thomas Daniel, London 1777, 12⅛ in. (31 cm)

3 Historical Background: servers in the eighteenth and nineteenth centuries

A brief outline of the historical stylistic background of broad-bladed silver servers will help to put the contemporary collection in focus.[1] These implements were intended for the service of fish, cakes, pies, puddings and other dishes. The term 'slice' encompasses a variety of shapes of broad flat utensils. Their history starts around 1700, when the development of table cutlery and the refinement of dining practices took on a new elaboration, stimulated by the social and cultural influence of Louis XIV of France. Until 1900 their design followed well-established patterns. Those in Britain preceded America by a dozen or more years.

In Britain, virtually all slices were triangular in blade shape until the mid-1770s and had the general conformation of the flat-bladed trowel. They are lifters rather than cutters, and were so used, for example, for the service of whitebait. The handle is attached to the blade by a decorative boss or bolster, and lifts on a stem above the plane of the blade. Initially, handles were principally of wood or ivory (fig. 1), later becoming more or less elaborate variations on contemporary silver cutlery designs (figs. 2, 3). The major variation consisted in the degree of rounding of the shoulders of the blade (fig. 2) – earlier ones were more severely triangular than later ones – or in its piercing, chasing or engraving, more or less elaborate depending on whether it followed Rococo (fig. 2) or Neoclassical style (fig. 3).

In the last quarter of the eighteenth century the favoured British form was a slim, flat, long oval (fig. 4), which, during the 1790s, merged with the scimitar (or falchion) knife shape; they were cutters as well as lifters. These long oval servers almost invariably had silver handles of the filled type: mechanically fabricated thin hollow handles that were filled with a siliceous-shellac cement into which the tang of the blade protruded. The handles might be decorated with stamped beading, shells or other designs and were oval, rectangular, hexagonal or octagonal in cross-section.

Finally, from 1800 and well into the twentieth century the scimitar shape prevailed with only some minor variations. They were primarily cutters. The right side of the blade is frequently characterized by two inward cusps, and the blade itself is dished (fig. 5). Changes of style referred only to recurring cyclic emphasis on geometric or naturalistic themes and the quantity of engraving on the blade. The Baroque and Rococo revivals that were in vogue during much of

A knowledge of that which has gone before is an essential springboard for the departure of the new

Justin Richardson

the nineteenth century often resulted in eclectic decoration. After about 1850 servers, whether for fish or cake, were more frequently made in pairs – fork and knife – and the distinction between their intended use disappeared as the blades became flatter, narrower and more knife-like (fig. 6).

American production tended to follow the British example, notwithstanding some characteristic stylistic wrinkles and Continental influence. Only a few trowel-shaped examples have survived; long oval shapes were practically non-existent, but the scimitar shape was plentiful. When American manufacturers became more dominant in the second half of the nineteenth century, the scimitar blades sometimes became frivolous in form (fig. 7). The firms of Tiffany and Gorham produced some of the most distinctive and distinguished servers of the late nineteenth century, as did Schiebler and a few others (fig. 8), notably in the Japanese/Aesthetic style.

Servers made on the Continent were both earlier and freer in stylistic expression than British examples (fig. 9). The trowel examples dating from the first decades of the eighteenth century, in Baroque taste, were more elaborate than the British. Handle shapes included the so-called cannon-end, which, although used in ladles, spoons and knives, never appeared on British broad-bladed servers (fig. 10). Dutch servers of the 1730s featured the triangular trowel, probably for cake (fig. 9), and an oval blade that was attached in roughly planar conformation to a silver handle, which were lifters for the service of fish, their function usually symbolized by elaborate piercing (fig. 11). Whereas Rococo influence was only timidly displayed in British servers between 1750 and 1770, it was fully expressed on the Continent at least a decade earlier, and persisted beyond the

... a door facing to the past and to the future, pulling together old threads into new, and sometimes not so new, patterns ... Wally Gilbert

end of the century (fig. 12). Production of trowel shapes and scimitar forms continued into the nineteenth century but long oval forms were not strongly represented. Scimitar blades differed in two respects from British and American examples; many Dutch, French and Portuguese servers had blades that were

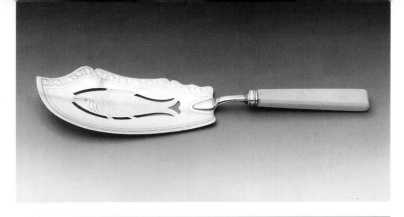

several inches longer and wider, and large, exaggerated, positive cusps were a prominent feature during the first quarter of the nineteenth century (fig. 13). Unfortunately, social historians have not been able to explain many of the details of usage that led to such changes in shape with place and time.

I am one in a living 'chain', a metalsmithing tradition stretching from antiquity into the future

John Cogswell

It is illuminating to realize that even one type of object, whether server or teapot, can reveal a history not only of style, but also of economic and cultural evolution. The threat to handwrought silver from mechanized commercial manufacturing began in the mid-eighteenth century with the development of Sheffield plate. Manufacturing methods were developed to manipulate the new sheet, the steam engine was utilized and machine methods of piercing, cutting and stamping increased. Instead of the laborious raising process, large sheets could be efficiently and uniformly rolled and formed into a variety of objects. Today, silversmiths cheerfully use lathes (as did the Romans), milling machines, presses and the like, as well as traditional methods such as hand-raising and casting, for the making of one-of-a-kind, handcrafted pieces.

From top:

5 Joseph Taylor, Birmingham 1824
11 ½ in. (29 cm)

6 Elizabeth Eaton, London 1847
13 ⅛ in. (33.3 cm) and 10 ¼ in. (26 cm)

7 James Watt, Philadelphia *ca.* 1875
12 ⅓ in. (31.5 cm) and 8 ⁹⁄₁₀ in. (22.5 cm)

8 Bailey, Banks and Biddle, Philadelphia 1878–94
12 in. (30.6 cm)

Right: **9** Jan van't Hofken, Amsterdam 1734
11 ¼ in. (28.5 cm) (*courtesy J. Van Loo, Epse*)

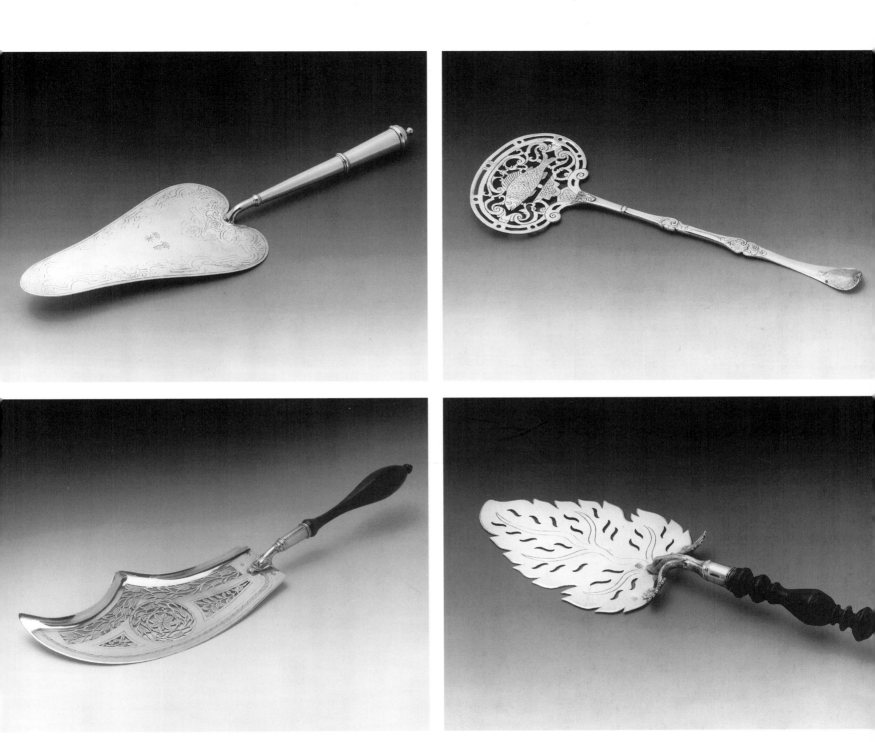

Clockwise from top left: **10** Gottfried Dubois, Stockholm 1723, 13½ in. (34.3 cm); **11** Matthias Lotter, Cape Town *ca.* 1747, 13½ in. (34.3 cm)
12 Bernard Wilhelm Heer, Kleve *ca.* 1780, 11½ in. (29 cm); **13** R.A. Verlegh, Breda *ca.* 1822, 14 in. (35.5 cm)

4 Silver Design in Britain and America: 1950–2000

Post-War Reconstruction

The first large-scale exhibition of contemporary, as opposed to historical, silver-work took place in London in 1938. Over thirty thousand people attended, portending a promising source of patronage.[1] The Second World War intervened, restricting the market and co-opting most of the skilled silversmiths into the armed forces. During the War the production of silverware was virtually stopped. Evolution in design was called to an abrupt halt in those countries most affected by the War, and the lead was taken by Scandinavia, notably Sweden and Denmark, where a strong tradition of contemporary design already existed. In Britain and America, the emphasis in metalsmithing was on forms based on 'Scandinavian naturalism',[2] while the organization of manufacture was balanced uncomfortably between craft and industry. As Eric Turner has remarked: "Neither any longer wholly craft nor yet exclusively industrial, the work of the [British] silversmith occupied an uneasy position between two extremes."[3] The beginning of the twentieth century had seen industrial production take over the role of the craftsman. "For the productivity-orientated industrialist, and for the technologist", explains Veronika Schwarzinger, craft manufacture had become "an obsolete economic model, and for the technologist, an antiquated production method".[4]

We set out to make works of lasting beauty, worthy of the finest materials Graham Stewart

The last fifty years of the twentieth century have witnessed the re-emergence and re-definition of the crafts.[5] The revival of silversmithing has involved a re-awakening of patronage from corporate clients and new educational institutions. This has been coupled with an increase in publicity via both traditional and new bodies. The Goldsmiths' Company, the Crafts Council and the new Association of British Designer Silversmiths in Britain, and the Society of North American Goldsmiths and the Society of American Silversmiths promote the craft in its broadest sense, through competitions, conferences and exhibitions (see chapter 7).[6] Small studio workshops are more able to survive alongside the big retailers such as Asprey and Tiffany, often supplying them with work.

After the end of the War, the silver trade was crippled by lack of demand. In Britain, this was exacerbated by the high rate of purchase tax levied on the maker's cost price to the retailer. The tax was at one time as high as 133%, so that an object that cost £100 to make was raised in price to £233, before the retailer's margin was added. In these circumstances silversmiths were unable to employ apprentices. It was in response to this situation that the Chancellor of the Exchequer introduced the Assistance to Craftsmen Scheme, whereby a piece approved by two panels of expert judges as a fine example of contemporary design and handicraft could be exempted from purchase tax. Under the scheme an item could be produced in a small edition – five repeats were permitted – but most were unique. These special pieces of silver had to bear the designer's name. Such names had previously seldom been given publicity, nor indeed had the names of the makers, except in the case of designer-silversmiths. The result was a blossoming of commissioning.

In Britain, the 1950s saw a burst of exhibitions, competitions and institutional orders for silver, coinciding with the emergence of a talented generation of designers and silversmiths supported by the Goldsmiths' Company. These included, in 1950, a contemporary silver exhibition at the Fitzwilliam Museum, Cambridge; in 1951, *British Silverwork … by Contemporary Craftsmen* at Goldsmiths' Hall; and in 1954, *Modern Silver*, also at Goldsmiths' Hall, which came right up to date with the inclusion of silver commissions from Leslie Durbin and others. The work of J.E. Stapley, R.G. Baxendale, Eric Clements, Robert Goodden, Reginald Hill and Cyril Shiner was exhibited alongside that of the young Gerald Benney and Alex Styles. The Goldsmiths' Company exhibition of 1954 was specifically intended "to stimulate interest in contemporary British silver; it will fulfil its purpose only if it succeeds in introducing designers to a wider circle of manufacturers and members of the public".[7] Every effort was made to cover the widest possible variety of styles and objects, with "both large ceremonial pieces, worth perhaps over a hundred pounds, and small things for domestic use costing no more than a new coat". The focus was on creating patronage.

The increased publicity and demand in turn led to an expansion of training in the 1950s. At the Royal College of Art in London, departments were reformed to provide for *both* industrial training and craft. Master silversmiths such as Leslie Durbin were employed as tutors, training young graduates such as Gerald Benney, David Mellor (who both graduated in 1953) and Robert Welch (who graduated in 1955), who went on to influence many of the present generation of British silversmiths. Their work, then as now, represents a successful balancing act between creating one-off pieces to commission for colleges, churches and private individuals and factory-made production pieces with international distribution.[8] The shift in interest from craft to design in Britain parallels that which took place in Scandinavia in the 1950s, and reflected a change of emphasis in support of product and industrial design, in response to the widening market of the 1960s. Some silversmiths proved both able and willing to design for stainless steel, plated wares and cast iron as effectively as in precious metal. Hence their names became common in discerning households which, though conscious of good design, could not afford, or did not want, silver.

> *My greatest pleasure is making the purely aesthetic, functional and technical aspects of design composition complement each other and work as one* Val Link

In America, the negative forces of the Great Depression, which created an antipathy against the industrial aesthetic, and of wartime trade embargoes, which initiated home-grown rather than European sources of luxury production, resulted in a positive growth of American craft and design.[9] Another factor in the American craft ascendancy was the influx of émigrés, many with a Bauhaus background, who came with a strong art and design heritage, but with few specific metalworking skills. Necessity, as ever, was the mother of invention, and aspiring silversmiths taught themselves innovative techniques that were to pave the way to an independent identity for American metalworking.

The American silversmith Kurt Matzdorf recalls that when he "entered the contemporary silversmithing scene in 1953, it appeared … to be almost a wasteland". By the early 1960s it had witnessed an exciting upturn. Summer workshops, organized by Margaret Craver just after the War, spread knowledge of Scandinavian styles and techniques, and many of the participants went on to become both metalwork teachers and some of the country's leading studio silversmiths.[10] An important element of the craft movement became university and college based when talented artists turned to teaching in the burgeoning higher-education network and financial independence led to greater freedom of expression. They felt a responsibility towards education, where ideas could be exchanged in a creative arena. This was a pivotal point in the transition from

> *I enjoy stretching the limits of convention for utilitarian objects, but it is important that each functions well* Cynthia Eid

apprenticeship to degree programmes, wherein metalsmithing was recognized as an art form. Simone ten Hompel believes that "the merging of silversmithing into metalwork [training] … was only possible within the open structure of the Anglo/American education system".[11] In America, design became an important part of student training, but with rather less emphasis on technique than in Britain. Many silversmiths turned to jewellery to supplement their incomes. Their customers, while being able to rationalize the purchase of items for personal adornment, found it less desirable to buy silver tea-services and tableware, reflecting both cost and a change in social custom. The choice of specialization within metalworking schools both in Britain and America shows a rise in silversmithing in the 1970s and a turn to jewellery in the 1980s and 1990s. The following table gives a summary of students graduating from the silver and jewellery department at the Royal College of Art in London. It reveals a bias among women to concentrate on jewellery, while more men became smiths. As silversmithing declined in the college, so the number of women in the department began to overtake men.

	Total no. of graduates	Silversmiths *		Jewellers		Total **	
		M	F	M	F	M	F
1950s	40	25	0	4	11	29	11
1960s	62	34	3	8	17	42	20
1970s	84	20	14	18	32	38	46
1980s	81	17	14	15	35	32	49
1990s ***	127					35	92

    *   Combined with Metalwork, introduced in 1986

    **   Breakdown by field not available for all years

    ***   1990 to 1998 only

Rod Kelly has summarized the present state of education in silversmithing that applies to both Britain and America:

> Today it is possible to become a silversmith in quite an academic way, studying design and craft, contrary to traditional training as an apprentice for a term of seven years. Depending on the individual's skill, the apprentice could hope to progress through the ranks of the trade … At art colleges today it is very difficult to learn technique in this way, although students are encouraged through design and workshop experience to have an understanding of most techniques. Silversmithing today is split between those who have a trade background and employ draughtsmen to design, and those, like myself, who have a background in design.[12]

After a slow start, the second half of the twentieth century has experienced a world-wide craft renaissance.[13] The craft of the silversmith is very much part of this revival, as new demands, new materials and new lifestyles inspire committed individuals to develop strategies for expression and survival. The source of today's progressive design has polarized. It is either in the hands of the owners of small craft workshops or lies within the realm of a few distinguished large-scale manufacturers, for example the San Lorenzo workshop in Italy.[14] The growth of the former is a world-wide phenomenon of the last five decades: witness the exciting silverware emerging from Japan and Korea, and also from Australia. Part of this interchange involves the dissemination of such metalworking techniques as *mokumé gané* to Western silversmiths. Development and expansion has involved the reconciliation of many apparent paradoxes, between hand and machine, the unique and the multiple, art and craft, tradition and innovation, and the precious and the everyday. Martin Eidelberg's comment on American metalwork also stands for the situation in Europe, where "It is not easy to define post-war style (in general) for there were a number of concurrent tendencies … The post-war period saw a juxtaposition of opposites".[15] For Britain, Marina Vaizey sees silversmithing as "characterized by outstanding individuals, each contributing very individually to the development" of the craft.[16]

> *The challenge becomes one of accepting the opportunity to design within the set limits*
> William Frederick

Contemporary silversmiths, however, are clearly the inheritors of past design movements. The three major currents that have preoccupied designers, craftworkers and historians during the past five decades are an increasingly concerted craft movement, the late stages of Modernism, and a decisive reaction against Modernism. Each working silversmith has negotiated their own particular pathway. Many see the challenge for contemporary silversmiths in the need to refine or define the use of new materials and techniques without the loss of traditional values.[17]

Looking Back to Move Forward: The Arts and Crafts Revival

The Arts and Crafts Movement under the guidance of William Morris in the second half of the nineteenth century had sought to achieve a regeneration of social and aesthetic values through a revival of the crafts.[18] Charles Robert Ashbee attempted to translate the ideals into practice, through the Guild of Handicraft established in 1888. Ashbee produced silverware with simple shapes, soft curves and a dull finish, shunning the high polish of traditional and machine-produced wares. These views were opposed to those of his predecessor Christopher Dresser, who designed functional objects specifically for mass-production and cheap sale. The firm of Liberty, founded in 1875, combined Ashbee's handmade look with the large-scale mechanical manufacture of Dresser's philosophy. The success of Liberty silverware was largely owing to the flair of its designers, such as Archibald Knox, and their understanding of techniques such as spinning and die-stamping used in its production.[19]

In British silversmithing today there is still a strong Arts and Crafts tradition, which has been passed from master to apprentice right through to the present day. Omar Ramsden had, in the first quarter of the twentieth century, evolved a style that blended modernity and traditional craftsmanship in a reaction against the excesses of mechanization. "Omar Ramsden stood by himself as a successful designer, craftsman and salesman. From his studio at St Dunstan's Place off the Fulham Road, he produced an atmosphere of *Arabian Nights* romance."[20] Leslie Durbin, a silversmith trained in Ramsden's workshop[21] as a chaser and decorator, and at the Central School in the 1930s, is a direct link with the last flickering of the Arts and Crafts tradition.[22]

Many British silversmiths, such as Rod Kelly and Michael Lloyd, find inspiration in that same Arts and Crafts Movement, often designing and making a piece from start to finish, concentrating on commissions rather than industrial design, and looking to nature as their source of inspiration. Lloyd, for example, confesses that he searches for a "great intimacy" with his natural surroundings; for him "the objective of work becomes a spiritual act, an act of thanksgiving for, and linking me to, my surroundings".[23] Many American silversmiths, such as Sue Amendolara and Helen Shirk, to name only two, follow the same philosophy of making. These silversmiths hold dear the idea of the medieval craftsman working personally on the design, manufacture and ornamentation of a commission, according to pre-industrial methods of organization. Handwork in the form of detailed naturalistic embellishment is a marked characteristic of their work. In the cause of the handmade, the latest technology and ceaseless experimentation are allied to respect for and understanding of traditions.

> *The satisfaction of being both designer and maker is due to the creative process not being limited to paper, but extending into the execution* Lucian Taylor

The Arts and Crafts approach to craftsmanship is, however, only one of many that inform silversmithing today. Eclecticism is more often the dominant source of invention. Some American silversmiths are more inclined to follow a somewhat 'hyper'-stylistic tradition that is both eclectic and fanciful. The craft movement has in many ways found its greatest acceptance in America, where it saw the growth of two related approaches: those who continued the long tradition of making functional objects, and those who branched out to create non-utilitarian objects as works of fine art.

Inheriting Modernism

At the beginning of the twentieth century the search for a totally new style of architecture and design took a radical turn in the birth of Modernism, with its ideological basis in functionalism. The application of Modernism to silver-smithing is clearly brought out in the words of the French silversmith Jean Emile Puiforcat (1897–1945), who virtually created the Modern Style in French silver in the 1920s:

> What we need today are utilitarian objects without ornamentation, that are not disguised as something else, although this does not prevent their being refined pieces of great value. The form imposed by its ultimate function is the object's permanent element. The desire to create a form of expression out of that form is what gives the object its constantly changing character.[24]

There were two main strains of Modernism. From the drawing-board and workshop of Henning Koppel at George Jensen came the long, flowing curves of Scandinavian Modernism, rooted in a long tradition of fine craftsmanship. Heikki Seppa, working in America but trained in Helsinki and at Jensen, promoted expression over functionalism. Hollow-ware became sculpture. Pattern and texture tended to be inherent to the material, and decorative ornamentation was almost completely absent. Scandinavian design, of which silver was a crucial element, achieved a synthesis of functionalism and humanism that became the visible expression of a distinctive design aesthetic. The other influential strand of Modernism grew from German approaches to function. The teachings of the Bauhaus reduced decoration to essentials, materials, functions and abstract relationships.

What you say is important – and what you say it with (the medium) must be used to its fullest Heikki Seppa

By the 1960s it was generally recognized that, whatever else Modernist design was, it was also a style. The dominant characteristic of Modernist design was simplicity. Ornament was eliminated, clean sleek forms were achieved at whatever cost to functional efficiency or 'honesty', materials were allowed direct expression, and historical references were outlawed.[25] The influential British silversmith Michael Rowe sets his work in the Modernist mould, and has explained why he believes it is still an appropriate and stimulating framework for creativity:

> in using the term Modernism, I am referring to a particular lineage of ideas that stretch back at least as far as the Enlightenment but which only blossomed in the early years of the century in response to the profound social and intellectual changes that occurred in Europe at that time. Central to Modernism is the idea that the artist's individuality is sovereign.[26]

Post-Modernism

Reactions to Modernism in silversmithing seem to be characterized by three different routes, two of which have been examined. The first was a return to Arts and Crafts ideals that pre-dated Modernism; the second was a continuing respect for Modernism; and the third was a rejection of precedent involving a variety of responses that can loosely be bundled together under the title of Post-Modernism.

The dissolution of the boundaries between decorative and fine art had its roots in the 1930s and 1940s. Movements such as Surrealism and Abstract Expressionism transcended the fine arts and entered mainstream design.[27] In an attempt to break out of the category of 'craftsman', silversmiths and other 'makers' moved into painting and sculpture in search of a new formal and intellectual basis for their work, a

I find more grace and elegance in a single line with the right curve to it than in a mass of the most intricate filigree Robert Farrell

direction often referred to as the Studio Movement. Momentous changes took place almost simultaneously through all the craft media in America in the 1950s, and within the next decade spread to Europe and Japan. Many artists moved away from a preoccupation with practical one-of-a-kind objects towards larger conceptions of their work as theoretical and serial. In America in particular, technique was given less importance than the intellectual concept of the object. Some artists, especially on the West Coast, began to assume a highly polemical and confrontational attitude in their work. Like the designers of the Arts and Crafts Movement a century earlier, Post-Modern practitioners assumed the role of the artist as reformer of society – reasserting the importance of the individual.

The Post-Modern Movement began in the crafts in the 1950s and became an aspect of the artistic and social unrest of the 1960s. The varied responses all involved a reassertion of the individual, and a search for a new humanism that was highly iconoclastic – pressed by the hippy movement and flower-power culture that flowed eastwards from San Francisco and which was followed by the age of activism. Jewellery-making became a dominant form in silver-smithing and a powerful vehicle for social and moral expression.

The most pronounced reaction occurred in Italy. Memphis, led by Ettore Sottsass Jr, was one of the first (founded in 1981) and most influential groups, with radical new concepts of form, pattern and colour.[28] As Barbara Radice, a founder-member of Memphis, comments, the group was "laughing out loud at our culture and at itself"; Memphis was "a kind of cartoon come to life – often satirizing the commercial styles of the 1930s, 1940s and 1950s, it pulls out the stops when it comes to colour, pattern, decoration and ornamentation".[29] Post-Modernists celebrate richness and complexity, form over function, the intuitive over the rational. Their work is characterized by use of exaggerated sculptural forms, liberated from functional constraints in an attempt to unite applied and fine art. Materials are used in surprising combinations. Silver-smiths, and particularly art jewellers, have since the 1950s subverted the doctrine of 'truth to materials' by using non-traditional materials and found objects. Some scratch and scour the surface, subverting the glossy sheen of polished silver, perhaps in an attempt to escape the élitist image of its past, when intrinsic value often overshadowed design and workmanship. Works that were silverplated only were admitted to the Triennale in Italy in 1986; supplementary materials such as acrylic resin, aluminium and wood, among others, were also permitted.[30] During these years the emergence of technologically driven manufacturing techniques such as the re-emergence of electroforming and the introduction of laser cutting invigorated the craft, shifting emphasis away from handmaking, which is now only one of many constructive and creative possibilities.

The challenge…is the need to refine or define the use of new materials and techniques without the loss of traditional values Marina Vaizey

For some, Post-Modernism is merely "a blip on the screen of the future". The American writer Lisa Hamel predicts a reconciliation between "the less-is-more economy of design (the old Modernism) … with a new sense of individuality".[31] Rosanne Raab summed up the situation in the final decade of the twentieth century in America, where "creativity, more than suitability for any preconceived function, is pursued by a majority of artists continuing the tradition of silversmithing in America".[32] The replacement of silverware by alternative, cheaper, consumer durables has meant that "The traditional necessity of production for use being largely dissipated, silversmithing is now free to pursue predominantly creative ends in their own right, to create autonomous forms beyond those bound by utility, free for the art of form".[33]

Into the New Millennium

The greatest challenge that silversmiths need to confront in the first decade of the twenty-first century is the changing nature of their market and the self-image of their craft. The impression gained from reviews, newspapers and articles is that, to potential consumers, silver is an antiquated symbol of status. Once bought as an investment, silver is no longer an attractive option. The modern family opts for stainless-steel flatware. Land, property, savings policies: all offer greater returns. The dining room has been replaced by the kitchen as the major status symbol room in the house. People pay extravagantly to equip and refurbish their kitchens, where once expense was lavished on the communal dining space. Status is conveyed through the possession and display of washing-machines, cookers, microwaves and freezers, through 'designer' orange-juicers and coffee-makers.

A small example of this spatial shift in the domestic interior is the fate of the napkin-ring, which is now "an endangered species". The napkin-ring is an "object that has been neglected to the point of extinction". As families eat together less and less, at breakfast bar rather than at table, where paper 'serviettes' have become acceptable at all but the most formal of meals, this example of the silversmith's craft has been marginalized.[34] How ironic that its size makes it affordable and its shape an ideal vehicle for inventive construction, decoration and personalization.

"Silver", writes one reviewer, "carries with it many associations. It is the stuff family heirlooms are made of, it gets stolen, it gets sold when times are hard and (if there is any left) it gets polished up for special occasions … All this adds up to an image which is deeply staid, a craft more adept at reproducing old patterns than at exploring new design directions."[35] This in fact is a complete reversal of past example, when silver was in the vanguard of design, other materials such as ceramics following its form. Silverware was never static; it was constantly being recycled, refurbished, refashioned to conform to the latest style. As the 1950s began with a spate of exhibitions to publicize the craft, so in the years up to 2000 the number of shows focusing on it increased. These promotional events tend to concentrate on either the appropriateness and affordability of silver, featuring batch-produced as well as commissioned objects,[36] or the idea that silverware is 'art'.[37]

The object should express itself and not a related subject. It should exist and be celebrated in its own right Chris Knight

The problem of positioning the craft of the silversmith between the fine and decorative arts is a major issue. For Martha Sung-Won Lee, who teaches silversmithing in Korea, the function of the object sets it above, not below, the fine arts. Upturning the accepted hierarchy of the arts, she argues that:

> The objects from the fine arts are attractive as room decoration, but they are not absolutely necessary. Their absence does not make life uncomfortable. However, the utensil cannot be separated from the person because it is a tool at his or her service. A person needs it.[38]

Jack Lenor Larsen has suggested that:

> … silver vessels are the jewelry that punctuates a room. In a world too seldom enriched by ritual, a silver teapot can make teatime more memorable. Life, after all, is not so dissimilar from theater where props are important to both. If we are not princes in our personal spaces, where else will we feel this privilege, or enjoy such small gleaming reflections of an enhanced life-style?[39]

The exciting and challenging solutions that today's silversmiths are producing reflects their own varied background and training. Phillip Baldwin, for example, was trained in blacksmithing (as was ten Hompel) as well as sculpture, while Wade Callender began life as a chemist. Many silversmiths produce jewellery in tandem with hollow- and flatware. The juried competitions first organized by Fortunoff in America in 1989 encouraged submissions exemplifying traditional skills, modern technology and mixed metals. The boundaries between materials and disciplines have been crossed, allowing a free flow of ideas. There is no all-restricting stylistic norm.

The ductility and malleability of metals – silver and gold – are [their] strongest characteristics

Heikki Seppa

Design in the 1990s is fragmented, with no one particular ideology or movement to steer the course. Given the multiplicity of approaches adopted by contemporary silversmiths, it is difficult to see any clear categories. In the end, however, contemporary craftsmen and women are never easy to classify, and most would reject the labels that writers in search of connections and continuities place on them. Silversmithing, as Simone ten Hompel eloquently explains, "is a language in its own right, without using words".[40]

5 Looking at the Collection

The diversity of the collection presented in this book stems from the deceptively simple design brief to each designer-maker, to "supply a server". The range of responses to this brief reveals the triumph of individuality, a just reward for any patron who commissions without creative constraint. This freedom has provided an all-too-rare opportunity to catch a very personal glimpse of the silversmith's mind and hands at work, without the usual compromises of cost, client or even function. As a result, this collection of over sixty servers represents an opportunity to review the state of the craft at the end of the last century and to find dominant influences through the diversity of interpretations.[1]

After a century of crisis for the craft, it is heartening to see that designers and artists are still drawn to silver as a means of articulating their ideas. Many of the makers have expressed a close identification with the metal. Through their work, silver has maintained its role in the world of art, craft and design. The inherent qualities of the material, most notably its malleability, offer almost limitless opportunities for experiment, the metal moulding itself to the maker's will. It is an ideal material to express movement, a common theme running through the contributors' statements. Out of this admiration for the metal appear three clear dualities, which cross boundaries of age, country and training: the forces of austerity and opulence; the demands of function and fine art; and the tensions between tradition and innovation.

As an intrinsically valuable material, silver has always been associated with wealth, which has helped distance it from a more general public. In order to reach this wider public, some silversmiths etch and oxidize the surface of their work in denial of a reflectiveness that echoes the brash shininess of a past age. Others choose to celebrate this quality and make it relevant to a modern audience.

For most silversmiths function played an important role in the realization of their commission. Far from being seen as a constraint, concern for function is a spur to creativity. Even those makers whose work seems to fly in the face of practicality have function in mind when they design: experimenting to see how far they can go, pushing the boundaries even further. Seen in this way, a concern for function should not be set against the sculptural qualities of silverware, but as an integral part of its realization.

One of the biggest challenges for the contemporary silversmith is to balance traditional techniques of manufacture with innovative design ideas, processes and materials. For some, such as Angus McFadyen, Ronald Pearson, Alfred Ward or William Frederick, the mastery of traditional methods of production in itself perpetuates that tradition. The pursuit of tradition need not necessarily be seen in opposition to innovation, however. John Marshall works within a traditional frame of reference to achieve startlingly avant-garde work. Simone ten Hompel achieves a balance between making unique pieces and the pursuit of basic forms that can be "easily repeated for facility of commercial manufacture".

The collection includes pieces that demonstrate a fine mastery of the ancient elements of the silversmiths' craft. The servers of Robert Butler, Kevin Coates, Martin Baker and Michael Brophy are virtuoso pieces of casting. Malcolm Appleby, especially, and his students Graham Stewart and Angus McFadyen, demonstrate the art of engraving. Rod Kelly and Michael Lloyd use their servers as vehicles to demonstrate their outstanding skills as flat chasers. The technical brilliance of Ros Conway and Jane Short's enamelling demands attention. In the work of Alistair McCallum, Roger Horner and Phil Baldwin the techniques of *mokumé gané* combine a complicated decorative process, Oriental in origin, with Western forms. While some silversmiths have pushed traditional techniques to the height of sophistication, others attempt to create new effects through experimentation, for example Julia Woodman's three-dimensional tessellation on the handle of her server, or Adrian Hope's process of paper embossing.

The creative tension between tradition and innovation is not only apparent in methods of production, but also in sources of inspiration, which draw a balance between past design solutions and current topics of reference. For most silversmiths inspiration does not come consciously from overt historical references, but from a percolation of ideas. Most, for example Justin Richardson and Alex Brogden, recognize a debt to the past. In some cases the source of the reference is explicit, as in the consciously Art Deco designs of William Frederick and Wade Callender. For others the direct source is a more covert empathy and, for such people as Roger Horner, pleasure lies in the confrontation of the traditional with the unexpected. Chris Knight is inspired by machine tools; his work is meant to attract and repel, leaving the viewer in a state of delicious confusion. The relationship between past and present is a complicated one, but out of complexity is born originality and diversity. It has been a revelation to see how some pieces apparently trail the heritage of centuries of stylistic development, while others seem to spring *de novo* out of present influences in art and society.

No simplistic dichotomy appears between the work of British and American silversmiths. There is somewhat more emphasis on surface decoration – chasing, engraving, enamelling – in British work, and concern for functionality. This reflects the long tradition of apprenticeship in British training, as well as the continuity in emphasis on utility that extends back into the centuries-long history of antique silver. There is, perhaps, a greater 'freedom' in the designs of Americans, which is also reflected in the work of contemporary potters; this may be a freer acceptance of conceptual rather than craft-orientated motives. In part, these differences originate in differing emphases in education and training – apart from employment factors. Metalwork departments in universities and colleges throughout America and the United Kingdom facilitate the development of greater individual expression. However, one need not pursue a search for national identity in these very personal responses to a broad brief. In fact, examination of the examples in chapter 6 reveals many instances of overlapping motives between the two cultures. Far from being a memorial to a dying craft, the collection is a testimony to its renewed energy and relevance to modern life.

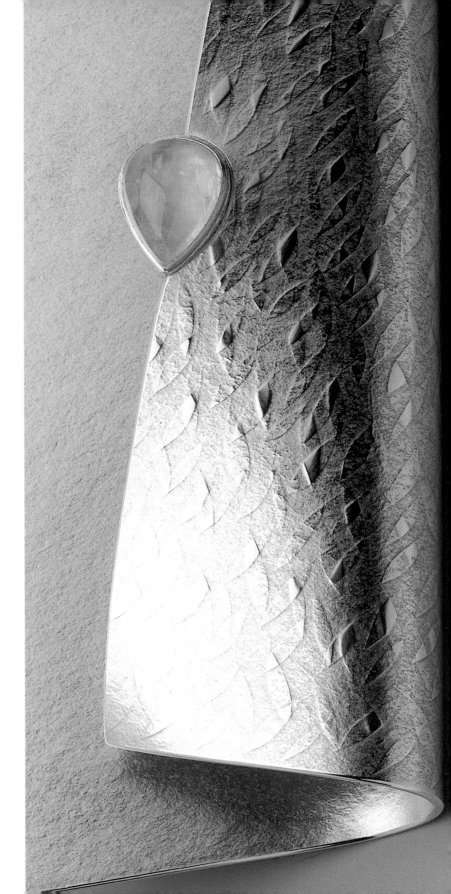

6 The Collection

British Silversmiths

pages 28–95

American Silversmiths

pages 96–153

The biographical sketches of the artists given in this chapter are necessarily incomplete and date from the time of writing. The passage of time keeps pressing them to new achievements. Nonetheless, it is hoped the details will be useful for the reader who wishes to find out about regular exhibitions, awards and degree shows, and the principal colleges for silversmithing. Contact the silversmiths through the organizations listed on page 158, where you will also find a note about colleges and galleries mentioned in the following text.

Entries for British pieces give the place and date of assay; those for American pieces list where and when they were made.

British Silversmiths

Malcolm Appleby
Brian Asquith
Martin Baker
Gerald Benney
Alex Brogden
Kevin Coates
Ros Conway
David Courts and Bill Hackett
Leslie Durbin
Anthony Elson
Wally Gilbert
Simone ten Hompel
Adrian Hope
Justine Huntley
Kay Ivanovic
Rod Kelly
Chris Knight
Michael Lloyd
Alistair McCallum
Michael McCrory
Angus McFadyen
Hector Miller
Jacqueline Mina
Peter Musgrove
Shannon O'Neill
Justin Richardson (and Steven Ottewill)
Toby Russell
Jane Short
Dennis Smith (and Gareth Harris)
Graham Stewart
Lucian Taylor
Alfred Ward
Julie Whitelaw

American Silversmiths

Suzanne Amendolara
Phillip Baldwin
Candace Beardslee
Flora Book
Michael Brophy
Robert Butler
Wade Callender
Chunghi Choo
John Cogswell
Cynthia Eid
Susan Ewing
Robert Farrell
William Frederick
David Gackenbach
Skip Gaynard
Roger Horner
Val Link
John Marshall
Kurt Matzdorf
Komelia Hongja Okim
Ronald Pearson
David Peterson
Harold Schremmer
Andrea Schweitzer
Heikki Seppa
Helen Shirk
Nancy Slagle
Julia Woodman
Kee-Ho Yuen

British

Malcolm Appleby

Cake slice
Sterling silver
Edinburgh 1990
Length 11 ¼ in. (28.5 cm)
Weight 14.7 oz (435 g)
The slice carcase was made by Peter Musgrove (q.v.)

The slice has something of the curling stone in its design; the solid forged handle loops forward before sweeping back. The decoration illustrates the remarkable engraving talents of the artist as well as his sense of humour. The heart-shaped blade is engraved with a lusty, earthy, gluttonous queen whose hair/tiara is in the form of a fleur-de-lis, symbol of the French monarchy. She clutches cake in both hands, and her earrings and jewellery drip cream cornets and other pastry goodies. Her ample body and dress have been artistically crammed into the available space and she eats the alleged words of Marie Antoinette, "Let them eat cake", which are engraved around the end of the heavily textured handle.

This slice is a bravura performance of interpretation and execution. The classic antique trowel shape is brought up to date and bears the artist's personal imprint on it. In a characteristically humorous approach, Appleby has interpreted the trowel as a spade for shovelling cake. The slice is also heart-shaped; the Queen of Hearts is also queen of tarts. The delight in this object is in its coded messages, which the user deciphers with amusement: the buxom monarch hidden in the elaborate fretted blade, until she is suddenly recognized. Playfulness and practicality are in no way incompatible, as Appleby proves, playing with ideas as well as with forms. He added a further personal touch for the commissioner by engraving a letter monogram R on the butt of the handle.

Artist's philosophy/statement: To paraphrase Appleby's characteristically succinct statement: he attempts to create a practical form whose decoration is related to function. In this case he incorporated the most famous cake quotation ever made. He admits to perpetrating "refined vulgarity" on occasion. He does seek to provide customer satisfaction! His sense of humour and scorn of pomp are as notable as his superb talents.

Born: West Wickham, Kent, 1946

Training and work: Beckenham School of Art, Ravensbourne College of Art and Design, Central School of Art, Sir John Cass School of Art, Royal College of Art. Started as an engraver in 1968. Set up shop in Crathes Station, Banchory, Scotland, in 1969, from where he has only recently moved closer to Edinburgh. A specialist gun engraver, he has created new approaches to silver engraving and techniques for fusing gold on to steel.

Appleby is a Liveryman of the Goldsmiths' Company.

He is one of the most outstanding British engravers and his rifle engravings are world famous. He is represented in notable public and private collections and museums, including the Royal Armouries and The Silver Trust 10 Downing Street Collection. There have been numerous exhibitions of his work, which includes the engraved orb in the coronet for HRH The Prince of Wales's investiture (on loan to the National Museum of Wales, Cardiff) and the Five Hundredth Anniversary cup of the London Assay Office. A major retrospective of his work was held in Aberdeen in 1998.

Malcolm and I first met in 1989 in the Fellows' Room of the Royal Society in London. He immediately impressed me with his trademark: a huge wool sweater (coat) of many colours, his ongoing project of many years, to which repair is made in any colour at hand. He undertook to send me a drawing some time in the next year, and the happy result is seen here. Malcolm is something of a character – a no-nonsense, direct individual with a wicked sense of humour. Although a Kentish man by birth, he worked and lived at the time in the old Crathes Station at Banchory, Scotland, where he was a valued participant in local social life. He still resides in Scotland.

Fish slice

Sterling silver

Sheffield 1997

Length 11 ¼ in. (28.5 cm)

Weight 11.9 oz (370 g)

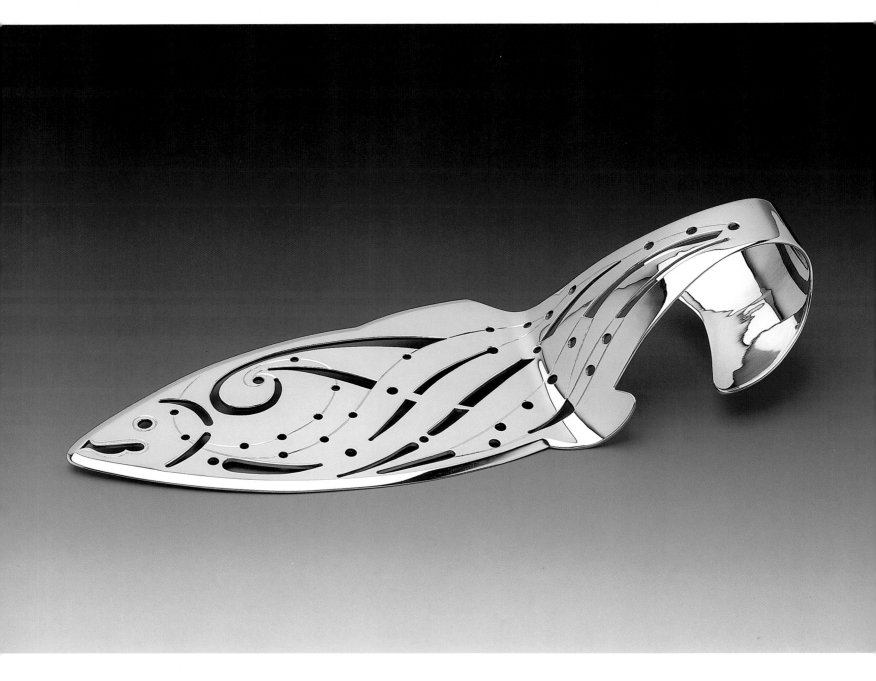

Brian Asquith

Asquith's server unites function and decoration in a stylish response to the design brief. Simplicity of form belies a keen knowledge of the material. By cutting, fretting, bending and polishing, a single sheet of silver has been given life and form. The handle arches up into the grasp, the tail flicked down to act as a support, but also as a focus of energy. The piercing creates both lightness and a sense of movement. This fish appears as slippery as its real-life inspiration.

Artist's philosophy/statement: "I have come to believe that the principles involved in design for mass production or for individual craft objects are compatible; that the differing approaches and techniques add quality to one another, giving poetic meaning to objects which transgresses their purely functional needs, challenging with new patterns of thought and giving hope for the future." Asquith enjoys the sculptural, malleable nature of silver. He is "excited by the idea of objects reflecting a great tradition" and "places emphasis upon a continuum in the objects of civilization, which embraces both craft and industry … The irony is that, given the current state of things, small craft businesses are the future of industry."[2]

The blade is in the form of a fish whose tail bends over to form the handle and rest. It is highly polished and is pierced and engraved with a fluid sweeping pattern of circles, scrolls and arcs. It displays a charming, pierced, toothed mouth. The decoration comes to the top of the handle arc. The blade is asymmetric with implied fins on both sides. The edges are heavily bevelled.

Born: Sheffield, Yorkshire, 1930
Training and work: Royal College of Art, 1947–51, under the Professor of Sculpture, Frank Dobson; National Service, 1951–53; set up independent design workshop in Sheffield, 1955; moved in 1963 to Youlgreave, Derbyshire, where he works with his three sons.

Asquith has received many awards, including six from the Design Council, the Milan Triennale Award and also the Silver Medal. Among other distinctions he is a Liveryman of the Goldsmiths' Company, Honorary Fellow of the Bolton Institute, member of the Crafts Council and Fellow of the Royal Society of Arts. He has contributed to the Lichfield Cathedral Collection and The Silver Trust 10 Downing Street Collection. Innumerable commissions for churches, cathedrals, colleges, museums, the Goldsmiths' Company, institutions, sports associations, government and companies. Many exhibitions at museums and galleries, including a retrospective at Goldsmiths' Hall, London, in 1993.[1]

I met Brian in September 1996 at a display of napkin-rings at Goldsmiths' Hall, London. A brief conversation, together with my awareness of his distinguished silversmithing accomplishments, led thereafter to this commission.

Fish slice
Sterling silver, partial gilt
London 1993
Length 12 ¼ in. (31 cm)
Weight 20.3 oz (631 g)

Martin Baker

The large blade is a casting of a realistically modelled crab whose great claw 'holds' the handle. The underside is also true to nature with the shell carapace and other oddments of anatomy. The up-curved handle is further unified with the blade by strands of gilded seaweed and barnacles.

Baker's modelling prowess is evident in this heavy 'Rococo' piece. Like his American counterpart Robert Butler (q.v.), Baker is a skilled caster, and has used this technique to create a striking server that centres on a crab, taken not only literally as the blade but also as metaphor, using the movement of the crab claw as inspiration. The sheer realism of the cast form seizes the imagination, and adds a thrill of drama to the act of serving; if you are not quick enough the menacing claw locked on to the handle might get you! Our appreciation of realistic modelling, 'captured from the life', ties this server to the cast marine creatures created by the French eighteenth-century Rococo silversmiths Thomas Germain (1673–1748) and Juste-Aurèle Meissonnier (1695–1750). Their tureens and sauceboats were topped by silver fishes, shells and crabs, some of them cast from life, and revelling in the same watery environment that Baker has drawn upon.

Artist's philosophy/statement: "I enjoy combining decorative themes with functional forms to create unique handcrafted pieces with a timeless quality. How to design a fish server that conjures up imagery of a water world without succumbing to the traditional representation of a fish was the challenge I set myself. Since I had always been fascinated by the structure and movement of crabs, I set one in front of me as my model. The most enjoyable part of the process was carving the wax replica of the crab. It was difficult to keep the carving thin and flat enough for the slice to be functional and also to achieve a three-dimensional look without losing detail. Carving in low relief produced the desired effect. I wanted to find a way to relate the modern contoured shape of the handle with the design of the crab. I was stimulated by the strength and power of the claws which I fashioned to grip the handle. To enhance the sea theme I entwined seaweed through the claws of the crab up along the handle, picking it out in gold plate. I completed the design by embellishing the top and bottom of the handle with barnacle shells."

Born: London, 1952

Training and work: Central School of Art, BA (Hons.), jewellery, 1973–76; Royal College of Art, 1976–79. Established workshop in Soho, London, in 1979 as a designer-craftsman in jewellery and silversmithing. Work for Liberty, London. Part-time tutor at Central St Martin's College, London.

Craftsmanship and Design Award, Goldsmiths' Company, 1983 and 1990. Numerous industrial and group exhibitions in UK and USA. Also exhibits at Wartski, London. His work is in the collections of the Victoria and Albert Museum and the Goldsmiths' Company. Commissions for HM The Queen, HRH The Prince of Wales and King Hussein of Jordan. Other commissions for Garrard, Tiffany, De Beers, Walt Disney and private collections.

I had seen examples of Martin's work previously in London. After proposing a possible commission, I met him at his studio – a walk-up perched high above a teeming market street in Soho – to discuss the idea in detail and to tell him about my concept of the collection. In the course of our talk he proposed a crab motif with a great claw holding the handle, which I endorsed with alacrity.

Gerald Benney

The blade of this trowel is a highly polished isosceles triangle that is decorated with a single circumscribing thread. The blade is bevelled along both edges. The junction boss is an oval tube that lifts to a horizontal hollow handle of oval cross-section. The handle is decorated on its upper surface with *basse taille*, a honey-coloured transparent enamel that reveals an engraved basket-weave pattern that echoes the finishing technique of wickering. The handle terminates in an upswept silver oval finial.

Benney uses precious metals, gemstones, enamel and hardwoods in his fabrications. His work usually displays one or more of several decorative features – polished silver forms, peened textured surfaces (called Bennellation!), and enamelled areas. This server illustrates the first and last of these. The style follows early eighteenth-century tradition. It is a highly functional implement of classic beauty, line and style, whose clean look harmonizes both function and decoration. It is timeless in its crisp simplicity and elegance of proportion. The woven effect on the handle, created by engraving and then floating enamel over the surface, is reminiscent of eighteenth-century wares whose handles were wickered to prevent the transmission of heat. This rich decoration of the handle is set off by the cool, polished geometry of the blade. The server stands firmly on the table, its handle raised to invite the grasp. As the doyen of British silversmiths, Benney has developed a distinctive style that is instantly recognizable in proportion, surface treatment and relationship to function.

Artist's philosophy/statement: "My philosophy as such is to project and involve my own personal design theme without too much reference to others in the field."

Born: Hull, Humberside, 1930
Training and work: Brighton College of Art, 1948–50, under Dunstan Pruden; Royal College of Art, 1951–53, under Robert Goodden. He established his first workshop in London in 1955 and moved to Beenham House near Reading in 1963. More recently (1995) he has re-established a shop in London. Served as visiting professor of silver-smithing and jewellery, Royal College of Art, 1974–83, where many illustrious students acquired their training or were taught under him.

Benney is a Liveryman of the Goldsmiths' Company, 1964, a Royal Designer to Industry, and a member of the Royal Society of Arts. He holds Royal Warrants of Appointment to HM The Queen, HRH The Duke of Edinburgh, HM Queen Elizabeth The Queen Mother and HRH The Prince of Wales. He has had numerous exhibitions and major commissions all over the world. He master-minded the commissions for the Lichfield Cathedral Collection, 1989–91. Awards and honours include two scholarships awarded by the Royal College of Art, in 1951 and 1953;

honorary degree, Leicester University, 1963; Freedom of the City of London, 1958, and the Borough of Reading, 1984; Hon. Fellow of the Royal College of Art, 1990; and Commander of the British Empire, 1994. He has held several important consultancies to government and industry at home and abroad.[3]

A rendezvous with Gerald in 1991 was an interesting experience. Professor Benney drove my wife (she would not forego the pleasure) and me the short distance from Reading station to Beenham Hall, a tastefully decorated Regency manor house in Berkshire – his then residence and workplace. The workshops where Benney's work group plied their skills were on the lowest floor. Some of his output carries the mark of an assistant – a generous acknowledgement of their contribution to the product. One of Benney's constant concerns is the preservation and advancement of the silversmith's craft.

Cake slice
Sterling silver and enamel
London 1992
Length 12 ³⁄₈ in. (31.5 cm)
Total weight 9.7 oz (300 g)

Alex Brogden

The blade is made from fourteen-gauge sheet, cut and filed on to a navette shape and bevelled on both edges. The rear portion is waved; the leading point is pierced with small wave forms. The handle rises on an aerodynamically, forward-pitched lift of shaped oval cross-section. It supports, under the leading quarter, a cast, symmetrical, pointed, elongated ellipsoid that is corrugated along its length with a wave form; the handle 'streams out' behind the blade.

Brogden's fascination with the reflective quality of silver, so well represented in his electro-formed 'ripple' dishes, is harnessed in this server to create an object balanced between movement and calm, lightness and strength, the organic and the geometric, and the natural and the man-made. This server captures something of the essence of Art Deco as well as a sense of speeding through water; its artful design also conveys a sense of flight – into the new millennium?

Artist's philosophy/statement: "This piece reflects my interests in the form and geometry of natural things. It is also designed to work well as a fish server. … The way that things grow and move, and the patterns generated by the interaction of elemental things – air, water, earth – intrigue me. I also enjoy the stylized abstraction of nature in ancient Egyptian and Greek architecture. … Making these forms in metal introduces light and reflections which can make static forms come alive."

Born: Rochford, Essex, 1954

Training and work: Nottingham College of Education, 1972–74; Ecole des Arts Marais, Paris, 1977–79; Bezalel Academy of Art, Jerusalem, 1981; Middlesex Polytechnic, BA (Hons.) 3-D design, 1979–82; Royal College of Art, 1983–86. Set up Ceramics Studio, Nottingham, 1974–77; Jewellery and Silversmithing Design and Workshop, London, 1985–89; Sheffield workshop, 1990–. Visiting lecturer: Camberwell School of Art, 1987 and 1994; Leicester Polytechnic, 1988; Royal College of Art, 1989–91.

Platinum Award for jewellery design, 1981; Royal Society of Arts travel bursary, 1984; Royal College of Art B. Yehia Prize for metalwork, 1986; Crafts Council selected index, 1990. Many exhibitions and one-man shows in England, Japan, France and Belgium. Many public and private commissions, including: Lichfield Cathedral Collection, The Silver Trust 10 Downing Street Collection, Goldsmiths' Company, Corpus Christi College, Cambridge, Crafts Council Collection, Shipley Art Gallery Collection, British Art Medal Society, Inchbald School of Design and the Honourable Society of the Middle Temple. Brogden has been the subject of reference or feature in many magazine and newspaper articles and books.[4]

I first met Alex over coffee at the Crafts Council in Islington. His work and style were already fairly well known to me through several exhibitions of work in the London area. We seemed mutually responsive and the result is the unique article shown here, which closely follows the drawing first supplied.

Fish slice

Sterling silver

Sheffield 1996

Length 14 in. (35.5 cm)

Weight 20.8 oz (647 g)

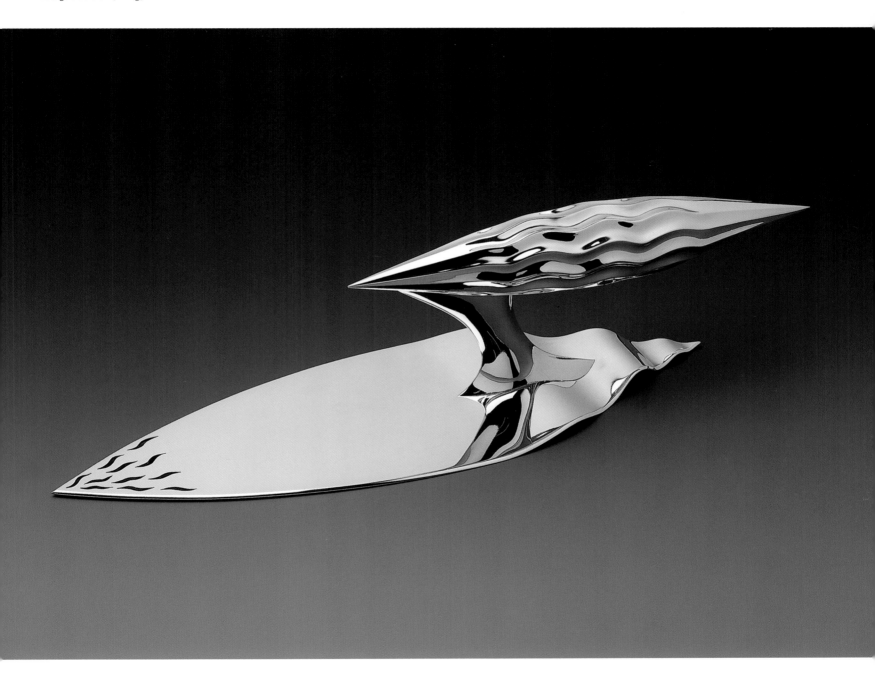

Cake slice
Sterling silver and agate, gilt
London 1992
Length 9 ½ in. (24 cm)
Total weight 11.5 oz (359 g)

Kevin Coates

This highly individualistic server has Coates's signature and the date *1992* inscribed on the back of the angel handle. A banded agate blade that has been coloured blue is held by the wings of a finely modelled cast angel, which forms the handle. The blade is trowel-shaped with rounded contours and is 4½ in. (11.5 cm) in length. It is ingeniously enfolded on the underside by the wing feathers. The handle is patinated and coloured by processes devised by the artist and which distinguish his work. A humorous play on words is provided by the inscription on the banner: *Panis Angelicus* (angel bread).

The server is an ornamental sculptural piece rather than a functional object. Coates's style is uniquely his own. If it has precedence, it is in the glories of the Renaissance. He seeks the essence of things in his life and his work. The piece brings out his fascination with allegory, with myth, and they are linked by him as he connects past and present. His work is drenched in meaning, a challenge and stimulus to the owner and user. In his combination of precious and semi-precious materials, in his skills as a modeller and technical virtuosity, he unites the craft of jeweller and goldsmith. He is perhaps the nearest thing we have to a medieval metalworker, whose work was sacred. His objects are jewels in their own right. Coates "carves his ideas in *materia dura*, producing visual music".[5]

Artist's philosophy/statement: Coates's inspiration derives from his inner emotions and sensitivity. "I approach all my output with what I see as the spirit of the jewel, whether it is to be worn, to be held and used, or placed on a table. Each piece is likely to have been initiated by my sense of wonder at some mystery, unresolved question, or phenomenon in either the natural world or the world of ideas, past or present. The pieces are realized by my forming connections of meaning, finding the resonance of linking cross-reference, and hopefully, an appropriate visual language by which to express them."[6] "A world-renowned goldsmith who brings to his work a panoply of diverse talents, he is a painter and sculptor, a musician and mathematician, a maker of musical instruments … ."[7] "The virtuosity of his carving, modelling and casting … explore[s] a rich world of allegory, symbolism, art and science."[8] "Outstanding in his ability to combine technical virtuosity with the visionary imagination of the true poet … ."[9]

Born: Kingston upon Thames, Surrey, 1950

Training and work: West Sussex College of Design, foundation studies, 1969–70; Central School of Art, diploma, jewellery design, 1973; Royal College of Art, jewellery design, 1976; Royal College of Art, PhD on the use of mathematics in musical instrument design, 1979; studied music, 1966–68, in Adelaide, South Australia, and continued independent study – a musician specializing in Baroque and early classical music and author of *Geometry, Proportion and the Art of Lutherie*.

Liveryman of the Goldsmiths' Company; Fellow of the Royal College of Art. Work in public and private collections world-wide. Important public commissions include the Peter Wilson memorial centrepiece for Leeds Castle; St Chad cup for the Lichfield Cathedral Collection; centrepiece for The Silver Trust 10 Downing Street Collection; Amity cup for the Goldsmiths' Company; Carrington cup for the Victoria and Albert Museum; and a paperweight for HRH The Prince of Wales. One-man exhibitions at the Victoria and Albert Museum, 1985, and Goldsmiths' Hall, 1991; and numerous exhibitions in UK and world-wide. First Marlow Award from the Society of Designer Craftsmen; first Norman-Butler Award, Goldsmiths' Company.

Kevin has proven to be a special bonanza – being a near-neighbour in London and, now, a friend. Being a very busy man, this piece was over two years in the making. His home with wife and fellow musical spirit, Nel Romano, has itself something of the quality of a jewel: his manifold talents are there revealed and encompass them in their daily life. He is a latter-day Renaissance man whose sensitive talents range beyond goldsmithing into the classics, mathematics, and a wide-ranging musicianship in Baroque stringed instruments, which he makes with consummate artistry and plays with professional skill.

Ros Conway

The server has a heart-shaped trowel blade. The rim encloses two engraved tiger prawns enamelled in yellows, blues and greens, incorporating some gold *cloisons* and separated by a central, barbed, longitudinal rib. The back of the blade was chased in a scallop-shell array by Michael Lloyd (q.v.) and is counter-enamelled in a muted *basse taille* yellow-shaded tone. The arched handle was electroformed in fine silver with a screw-shell terminal and is cold-pinned to the blade with a tri-pronged boss; it has a fine brush finish. The enamel has been ground to a matte finish and lacquered to protect the porous surface.

Although this implement bears a resemblance to the small trowel serving forms that were made in the latter part of the nineteenth century and early part of the twentieth (and which themselves had some models in English and, particularly, Continental eighteenth-century wares), this article is in a class by itself. This is a one-off stemming from the artist's inspiration. Conway, like Appleby (q.v.), has chosen the heart-shape form of trowel for her server, but for Conway colour is the driving force behind the design. The shape of the tiger prawns fits perfectly in the two lobes of the blade, their shimmering colour creating an almost *trompe l'œil* effect. The shell-topped handle recalls the elaborate and elegant cast ladle handles of the eighteenth century. While enamelling is some two thousand years old, invented as a substitute for precious stones, Conway's pieces are strikingly contemporary, and exploit the potential of enamelling to the point of its being an art in its own right, yet literally and metaphorically welded to the object. This is not a limitation but rather an integral motivation and inspiration for her work.

Artist's philosophy/statement: "I live and work on the water in a Rhine barge moored on the River Deben in Suffolk. Surrounded as I am by boats and the whole life of the estuary – fish and fowl – these have inevitably influenced my work. All these images have, however obscurely, crept into my work and so a commission involving fish was a gift. It gave me an opportunity to spend some time drawing and, inevitably, eating things fishy. When the design of prawns was chosen I did not want these to be a common pink or brown variety; instead I chose the lovely grey/green of tiger prawns with their subtle highlights. I asked Michael Lloyd, an old friend and oft-time collaborator on pieces of mine, to chase a cool and simple reverse as a contrast to the richness of the topside."

Born: Bristol, 1951

Training and work: Somerset School of Art, foundation year, 1969–70; Central School of Art, Dip. AD (First Class Hons.), 1970–73; Royal College of Art, 1973–75. Part-time teaching at Brighton Polytechnic and Epsom College; associate senior lecturer in jewellery, Middlesex University; visiting lecturer, Fachhochschule, Düsseldorf. Independent craftwork and enamelling from 1975.

Goldsmiths' Company Award, 1975; Sanderson Award for travel to Japan, 1976; British Craft Award; Northern Arts Fellowship and Crafts Council grant to study enamelling technique. Member of the British Society of Enamellers and Freeman of the Goldsmiths' Company. Numerous solo exhibitions throughout England and group exhibitions at museums and galleries in England, Scotland, USA, Germany and Japan. Many commissions for museums and public art galleries, including the Victoria and Albert Museum, Birmingham Museums and Art Gallery, Leeds City Museum and the Goldsmiths' Company. Conway has served or is serving on many panels, committees and councils of regional and national importance. She has been the subject of a number of articles, catalogues and other publications.

My wife and I met Ros at our London flat when she came to supper one evening after teaching. We learned of her interesting life with her husband and son on a barge, and of her teaching activities. She outlined her ideas for a small seafood server and we discussed options and preferences regarding the prawn ornament. Naturally, we agreed on the tiger prawns that she favoured.

Fish slice

Britannia standard silver, gold and enamel

London 1994

Length 9 ⅝ in. (24.5 cm)

Total weight 7.0 oz (217 g)

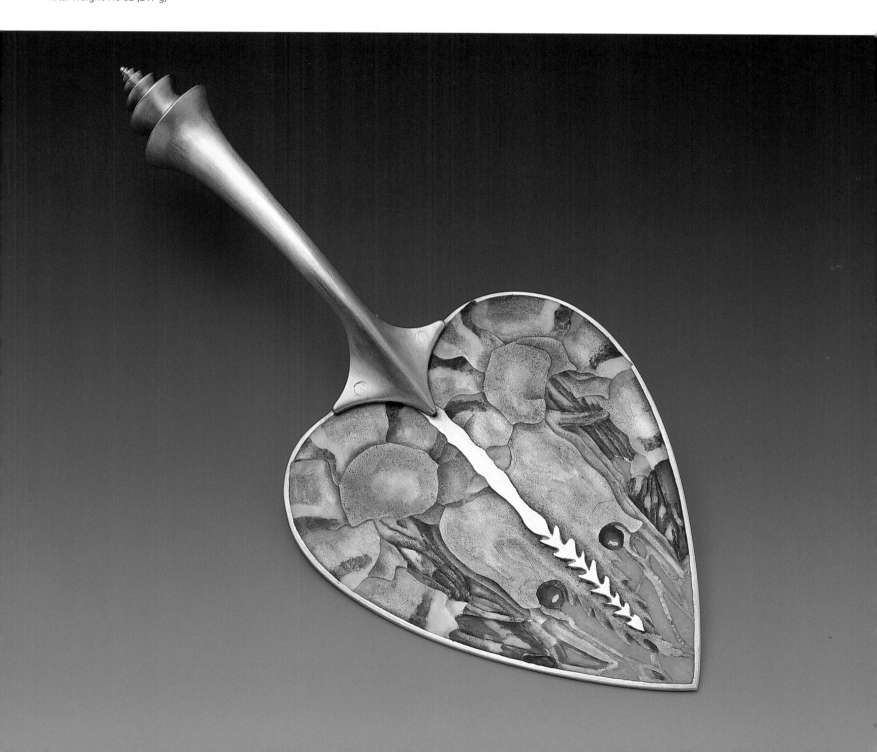

Fish slice

Sterling silver with 18k gold terminal bezel

that holds a large lustrous grey baroque pearl

London 1997

Length 10 in. (25.5 cm)

Total weight 9.7 oz (301 g)

The heel of the underside of the blade is inscribed

Designed by Courts and Hackett.

The server was fashioned by Charles Fowler,

a much-esteemed smith in commercial practice in London.

David Courts and Bill Hackett

The polished blade is of long oval shape with waved and sharply bevelled edges and claw-shaped heel. It is pierced and engraved over its whole extent with fluid comma and star shapes that are emphasized and extended by engraved arcs. The handle is a realistic fish vertebrae skeleton, which terminates in a pair of ribs. Vertebrae and ribs are accentuated by oxidized concavities.

The artists have laid bare the internal structure of this server. It is as if we see the skeleton of some aquatic beast. The crescent shape of the rib finial provides a visually startling impact as well as an admirably functional and stable means of supporting the implement. Anatomical fact is combined with fantasy in the gold-mounted silvery pearl that terminates the finial. The bold and forceful handle is countered by the pierced and flowing blade, which evokes the watery environment where this creature must have been born. We cannot be sure whether the skeletal handle is rising up or sinking back into the waves.

Artist's philosophy/statement: "It's all there in the natural world; just take the ideas and give them a good fit, a good feel and some sex appeal."

David Courts

Born: London, 1945

Training and work: Royal College of Art, MDes., 1971; Goldsmiths' Company Award, 1971; Freeman of the Goldsmiths' Company, 1983.

Bill Hackett

Born: Norfolk, 1949

Training and work: Royal College of Art, MDes., 1974; British Steel Award, 1974; Freeman of the Goldsmiths' Company, 1985.

Partnership in design and silversmithing established in 1974. Joint show, Wartski, London, 1976; group show, Victoria and Albert Museum, 1977. Commissions for De Beers Diamond Stakes; Victoria and Albert Museum; Goldsmiths' Company; MTV, Los Angeles; Goldsmiths' Company Prime Warden bowl. Featured in articles in books, magazines and newspapers in London, Norway and Japan.

I met David and Bill in their, then, attic workshop in Tufnell Park, London. It had a wonderful panoramic view of the City, including St Paul's Cathedral. I had earlier seen, in the Jewellery Gallery of the Victoria and Albert Museum, a technically and artistically wonderful bracelet made by them. We discussed the contemporary silversmithing scene over coffee and came to a meeting of minds on the present commission.

Leslie Durbin

The handle is a cast school of fish as is consistent with Durbin's prowess as a modeller. The fish dive into a flat sheet oblong pool that has a chased, waved and pierced surface. Naturally, Durbin executed his own decoration. The handle is both graphic and dynamic and surprisingly comfortable.

This slice is a new expression of the antique oblong shape of the late eighteenth century. In Durbin's interpretation of the design brief he has created a server that almost dissolves into the watery habitat which inspired it. The irregular and sinuous lines of the asymmetrical blade, with its fretted ripples, and the shimmering shoal of cast fish that form the handle, are united by serpentine lines that visually hold handle and blade together. The piercing of the blade and the linked fish, with space between, combine to make the server an airy object. But it is also very functional, easy to grasp, effective in use. The mixture of poetry of motion, skill in metalworking, originality of concept and firm grasp of function is the hallmark of one of the most respected silversmiths working today. He is also a living link with a distinguished metalworking heritage.

Artist's philosophy/statement: Durbin was one of the new and refreshing design spirits of post-Second World War British silversmithing. He is credited with maintaining "a fine balance between the traditional and modern trends in design"[10] – one "who perpetuates the great traditions of the past while creating their own. ... It is the individuality of design as well as the fine workmanship that sets [his work] apart". He states: "I try to include a personal motif appropriate to the occasion or the use."[11]

Born: London, 1913

Training and work: LCC Central School, 1926–29; travelling scholarship, 1939. Apprenticed to Omar Ramsden, 1929–38, as a decorator (chaser and engraver). Durbin further improved his silversmithing by attendance at Central School after work, and in his later education. He taught for a time at the Royal College of Art and at LCC Central School. He established his own workshop in 1945 in partnership with Leonard Moss. Among his many skills he is a specialist in modelling. His studio in Kentish Town was taken over by Hector Miller in 1976.

Goldsmiths' Company scholarships, 1938 and 1939. Member of the Royal Victorian Order, 1943; Commander of the British Empire, 1976; LLD (Hons.), Cambridge University. Stalingrad Sword and innumerable commissions for royalty, museums, public bodies and others, including design of HM The Queen's head for the Silver Jubilee commemorative mark. He was honoured by *Fifty Years of Silversmithing*, a retrospective exhibition held at Goldsmiths' Hall in 1982. In 1989 he received the Garrard Gold Medal for outstanding contributions to the trade.

An acquaintance with Leslie has been one of the signal privileges of this activity. We first met for lunch at the Royal Society in London to discuss a commission. Despite the accolades that have come his way he maintains a modest, if firm, manner. His strong design sense and fund of experience and ideas were soon evident. He quickly laid out what proved to be essentially the final design for his fish server – indeed he 'fished' some relevant castings out of his pocket. It was an enjoyable experience later to visit the garden workshop at his home in Kew. He well deserves the accolade bestowed on him by Cambridge University: "craftsman inspired by Minerva".[12]

Fish slice
Sterling silver
London 1990
Length 12 in. (30.5 cm)
Weight 14.4 oz (448 g)

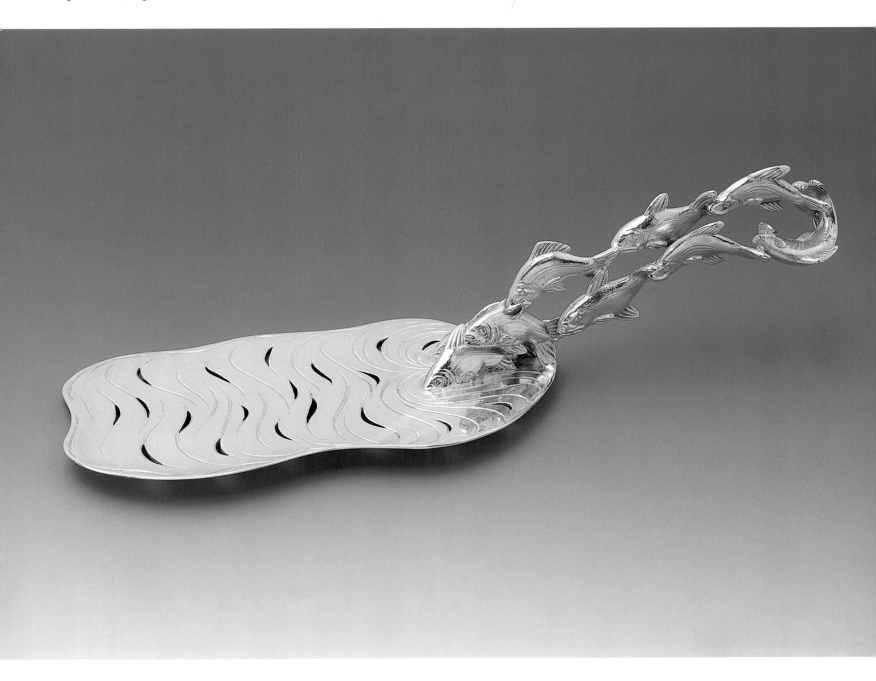

Anthony Elson

Fish slice
Sterling silver
London 1993
Length 12 3/8 in. (31.5 cm)
Weight 12.9 oz (400 g)

This server is in the shape of a deep-sea eel – a gulper *(Eupharynx pelacanoides),* which lives at a depth of one mile on the ocean floor. The cast body is heavily oxidized over a chased matte surface and has assumed the wonderful quality of black velvet. The fluted spinal, dorsal and pectoral fins and the eye are bright silver, as is a row of spots along the body. They provide exciting contrast. The tail has been brought back and loops to form part of the handle. The animal has an immense jaw – woe betide its victim!

With his deep concern about the diminishing range of skills within the industry, Elson's designs endeavour to combine these skills with rare imagination. One may see something of Art Nouveau in the disposition of the tail of this amazing creature, but it is a resemblance forced at least in part by the craftsman's necessity to fashion a handle from the body of the animal. The piece itself mirrors Elson's innate artistry and aesthetically original turn of mind, which finds no obvious precedence in stylistic history. The deep black surface, with its striking contrast to the polished parts, presents a beautiful surface property of silver that has rarely, if ever, been exploited so successfully before. This rich black creature seems to slither across the table; it has a life of its own.

Artist's philosophy/statement: In making a fish server, "I was determined to find a fish that had not been the source of inspiration for such an implement". This server reflects Elson's scholarship and original turn of mind – a fish server like no other.[13]

Born: Worthing, Sussex, 1935

Training and work: Brighton College of Art under Dunstan Pruden, diploma, 1956; Royal College of Art, BA, 1963; employed by William Comyns Ltd, 1964–68. Took over Blunt & Wray, silver- and brass-smiths, with a staff of up to twenty-five men making production pieces, 1968–81; founded Anthony Elson Silversmiths, 1981.

Silver Medal for geometrical decoration, Royal College of Art, 1963. Travelling bursary, 1964. Liveryman of the Goldsmiths' Company and past chairman of its Council for Craft, and service on the Council of City of London Guilds. Present workshop in Clerkenwell Green, London. Many prominent commissions from the City of London, London Stock Exchange, City livery companies, universities, corporations, Liverpool Anglican Cathedral and the King of Nepal. He has exhibited widely in UK, Europe, USA, Canada, Australia, and the Middle East, and his work is in many private and institutional collections.

It has been a pleasure to know Anthony. We first met in his studio near Clerkenwell Green in London, in a building inhabited by many craft and silver specialists. It is an area that abounds with metalsmiths. I knew of Elson's work, having acquired a marvellously chased coffee-pot a number of years previously in an antique shop; its deep-pressed rhythmic contours are both novel and striking. Elson turned out to be a reflective scholar with an interest in many aspects of learning and a genial, twinkling eye. He illustrates one of the many happy experiences of the associations formed in the act of collecting.

Wally Gilbert

The paddle-shaped blade and integral rolled handle consist of a pierced sheet to which heavy longitudinal wires and lighter binding wire have been attached. The whole was soldered by a granulation technique wherein a thin copper deposit is applied to the surface such that all contact points are in effect ready to be soldered by heating (sweating) of the whole; after this, excess copper is removed, the surface burnished, and the whole oxidized. This brief account is a gross simplification of all the time, skill and effort that were actually expended. The blade was hammered appropriately and a lifting edge rendered.

Gilbert's server is a fresh reappraisal of form, solving the problem of connecting handle to blade by making them one, weaving an object from metal wire that conjures up textile construction, Oriental cane kitchen utensils and fine English basketry. Its striking originality is matched only by the richness of the metaphor. Gilbert's server leaps across cultural boundaries and historical precedents. So much for the tendency of some art critics to classify works according to a current genre or to tie new works to a pattern of historic influence that excludes the independence of creativity as well as the universality and permanence of human conceptions of pleasing or good form.

Artist's philosophy/statement: "I [chose this technique] because I wanted the lines of the handle to flow unchecked through the blade and this would not be possible in casting. … This commission pushed me into attempting … a new and exciting scale of work in silver to my own design. … Any piece of work is a more or less successful partnership between the material and the designer-maker through the medium of the process." Gilbert further articulates this process in a way that reflects the sensitivity of the artist: "Throughout the design I thought about the papyrus boat construction methods in which bundles of reeds are sewn together. I looked at many stems of plants … and the folding of leaves. I pursued the resemblance between the wave pattern of the wire with ripples on water. … As with poetry, one is dealing with layers of association and reference to personal experience and cultural influences. Insofar as one aspires to be an artist or poet, one is Janus-headed, a door facing to the past and to the future, pulling together old threads into new, and sometimes not so new, patterns … through the medium of the material that he or she works with, whether it be words or sound or some other more tangible material."

Born: Cranleigh, Surrey, 1946

Training and work: Studied art and sculpture at West Sussex School of Art and Design, 1964–66, and Chelsea School of Art, Dip. AD, 1966–68. He changed his interest from sculpture as fine art (his father and grandfather were sculptors) to applied art. Taught part-time jewellery classes at several colleges since 1975. Worked with Louis Osman, 1982–89. He founded the Gilbert Studios in Marden, near Hereford. Has done production work but prefers one-of-a-kind commissions. Much previous activity has been in jewellery, although he is currently working on larger metal pieces, partly as a result of the present commission. Gilbert instructs blind students in silver craftsmanship at the Royal National College for the Blind in Hereford, having left Hereford College of Art and Design, where he had taught jewellery and art and design from 1978.

Gained West Midland Arts Grants in 1984, 1989 and 1996. Freeman of the Goldsmiths' Company. He is represented in many institutional collections, including the Victoria and Albert Museum, Birmingham Museums and Art Gallery and the Goldsmiths' Company. His work is shown in many prestigious commercial galleries in the UK and USA, and he has had many solo and joint exhibitions of his work around the world. He has published a number of articles on concepts and techniques in books, magazines and newspapers.

Wally and I met in 1992 at a preview exhibition of his latest jewellery at the Electrum Gallery in London. I was struck by his innovative technique. Our acquaintance has improved with time and contact into, for me, a sense of friendship. He very generously offered a number of drawings for election. I am pleased that this commission has, in part, helped to rekindle his interest in making larger wares.

Server
Sterling silver
Birmingham 1993
Length 14 ³⁄₈ in. (36.5 cm)
Weight 11.4 oz (355 g)

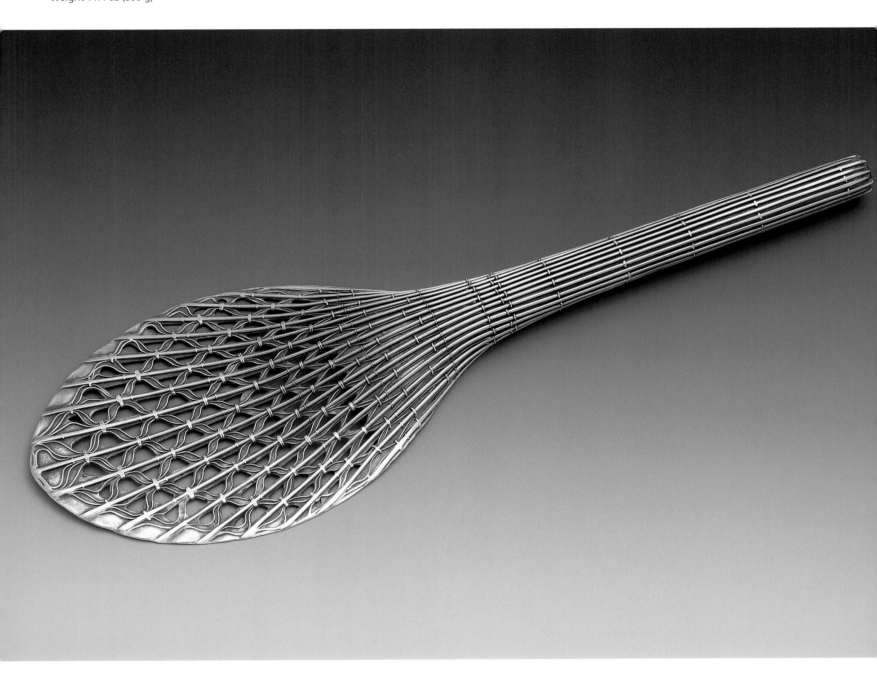

Cake slice

Sterling silver with gilded recess in handle

London 1993

Length 14 ½ in. (37 cm)

Weight 11.2 oz (348 g)

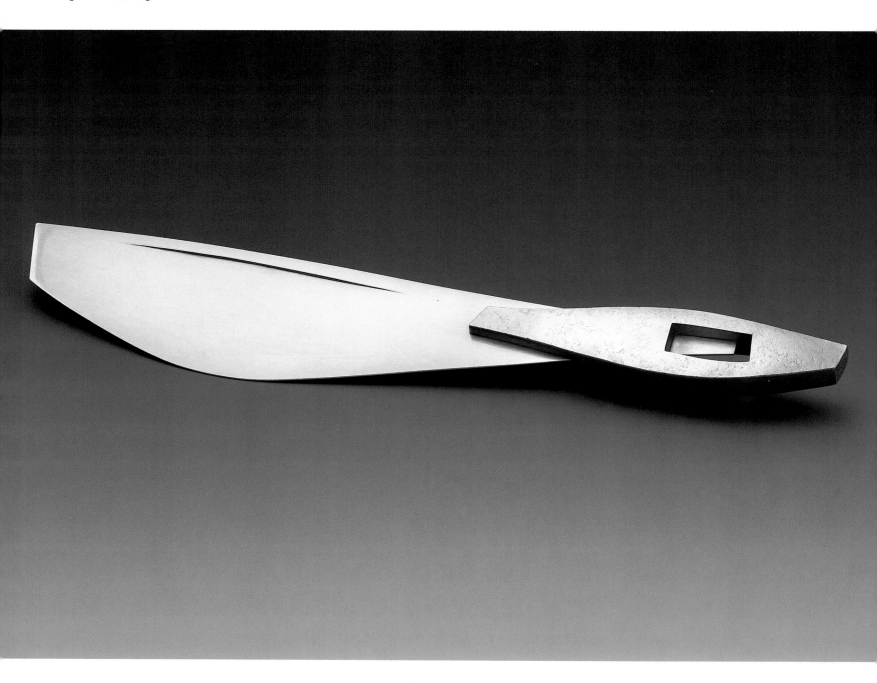

Simone ten Hompel

The blade is a long forged knife shape with the tip cut off in reverse of the scimitar. It has the unique decorative and strengthening feature of a displaced and soldered cut that runs along the rear edge of the blade. The tang of the blade is inserted into a slot in the handle and protrudes into a gilded slot in the squared 'oval' handle. Both blade and handle are textured and have a matte finish.

The minimalist character of this piece reveals much more detail on closer study. For Simone, form is ornament, and involves not only shape and outline but also texture. "On the surface her work may appear cool and puritanical but the simplicity of its lines cannot hide its intrinsic emotional qualities … This quality of her work becomes readily apparent when one observes the richness and subtlety of the surfaces and interior spaces. There may be no obvious ornamentation on the surfaces but there is a richness present which undermines the formal austerity. Her work is about forms and lines which come together in harmony."[14] Silversmithing, as she explains, "is a language in its own right, without using words".[15] She uses simple geometric shapes and revealed construction to speak to her audience – a personalized modernist vocabulary.

Artist's philosophy/statement: Ten Hompel produces designs in which the basic forms can be easily repeated for facility of commercial manufacture. Further variations, either by the addition of new elements or choice of metals and surface treatment, give each new version its own sense of exclusivity.[16]

Born: Bocholt, Germany, 1960

Training and work: Trained as a locksmith/blacksmith, 1975–79; studied jewellery at Fachhochschule, Düsseldorf, 1979–85; Royal College of Art, silversmithing, 1987–89. She combines teaching at Sir John Cass School of Art and Camberwell College of Art with creating in her own workshop in north London. She also writes on the subject of silversmithing.

Second prize, Junges Hardwerk, NRW, 1984; Garrard Award for Design in Precious Metals, 1989; Crafts Council grant, 1990. Solo and group exhibitions at Liberty, London; The Scottish Gallery, Edinburgh; Crafts Council of Ireland, Dublin; Antwerp; Crafts Council, London; Contemporary Applied Arts, London. Her work is in the collections of the Victoria and Albert Museum, Goldsmiths' Company and other museums, galleries and institutions.

I met Simone at an evening preview of metalwork at Contemporary Applied Arts, London. A visit followed to the subterranean depths of the workshop in Clerkenwell Green that she shared at the time with Rebecca de Quin and Richard Vallis. Simone eventually furnished four or five drawings of her concepts and, since she likes to work that way, several cardboard constructions of the piece.

Adrian Hope

The blade shape is intermediate between a long oval and a round-shouldered trowel. The blade has been pressed into an all-over wave pattern with many gold fish in silhouette in the waves. The blade edge is chamfered by chasing down from the embossed section. The raised embossed waves function as a draining-board and make piercing of the blade superfluous. The handle has the same pressed pattern and fish forms as the blade. It carries a heavy longitudinal rib on the top centre side, characteristic of Hope's use of rib joints in his panel structures. The handle, of roughly triangular cross-section, rises from the rear of the blade on a waved boss structure that matches the blade pattern.

This server is a modern interpretation of the eighteenth-century trowel. Panel construction in Britain goes back to the middle of the eighteenth century, to power stamping and other processes that came to the fore, especially in the fabrication of Old Sheffield articles. But Hope lends a new dimension to the technique with the beautiful ribbed effects that are prominent in his work. This server is about rhythm and flow. The fish beneath the waves give it a hidden depth; they swim down the handle and into the pool-like blade. This freedom of movement is controlled within a clear geometric form. As Adrian confesses, "Sometimes the idea comes from the metal, from the process, sometimes from the many sketches and drawings, but it is the eventual form that should tell its own story."[17]

Artist's philosophy/statement: "The technique that I am developing – paper embossing – is unusual in that pattern texture is achieved prior to any forming or assembly processes. This ensures a design discipline that, in turn, generates a new sort of freedom." *(adapted from original)*

Born: Edinburgh, 1953

Training and work: Sheffield College of Art, Hons. 3-D design; Edinburgh College of Art, postgraduate diploma, 1980. Worked in partnership with his wife, Linda Lewin, as designer/craftsman at the Gold and Silver Studio in Bath. They established a joint studio in Edinburgh in 1980 and moved to Stobo, Peeblesshire, in 1994.

Goldsmiths' Company graduate apprenticeship (Sheffield); first prize, silversmith design, Incorporation of Goldsmiths of City of Edinburgh, 1984, and Design Competition winner, 1987; Scottish Development Agency fellowship, 1988; Freeman of the Goldsmiths' Company, 1989. Exhibitions in Scotland, England, Ireland, France and Germany. Work in collections of Scottish Craft Collection, Royal Scottish Museum, Aberdeen Museum and Art Gallery, Bristol Museum and Art Gallery, Glasgow Museum, Goldsmiths' Company and others.

Adrian and I met at a fair in Goldsmiths' Hall, where his striking 'rib' technique commanded immediate attention. A wonderful large basket made in this way is part of the Goldsmiths' Company collection and graced a luncheon table when I had the pleasure of eating at the Hall. Adrian has continued his exploration of technique, including the fabrication of a small vase that has three external vertical ribs, split and fluted.

Fish slice

Sterling silver and 18k gold

Edinburgh 1995

Length 11 5/8 in. (29.5 cm)

Weight 9.2 oz (286 g)

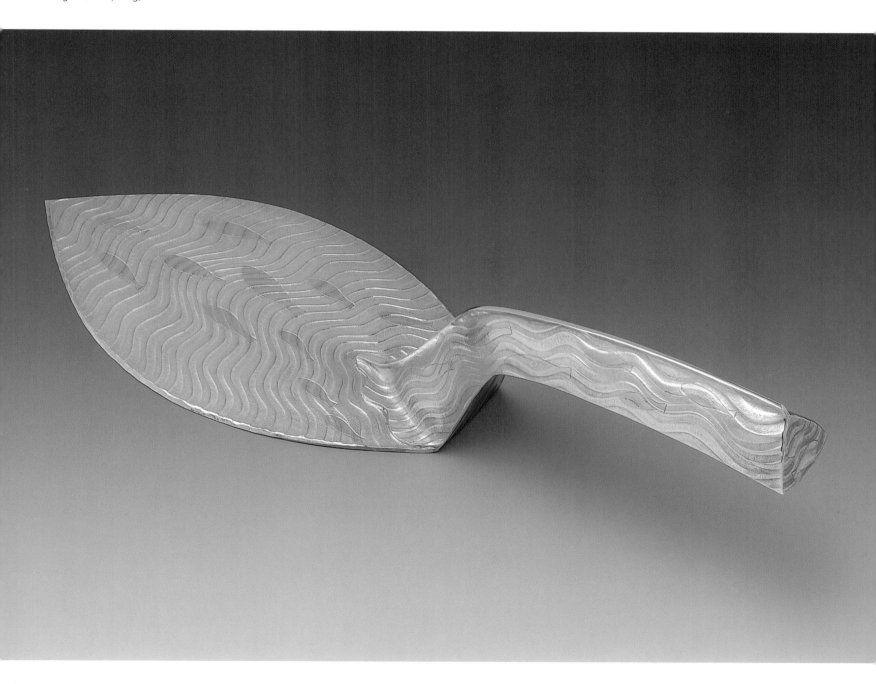

Cake slice

Sterling silver, 18k gold pin

London 1995

Length 13¾ in. (35 cm)

Weight 8.2 oz (256 g)

Justine Huntley

The blade is a broad asymmetric forged knife shape with a slanted flat leading edge and is vaguely reminiscent of a scimitar shape. The left and leading edges are chamfered. The rear edge of the blade breaks up into a slanted apron with a maximum height of 3 cm. The handle consists of two square rods of uneven length, 4 mm on each side, that pass through the apron and are tied together by a spiral roll of approximately twenty-four-gauge silver sheet and held by a gold pin. The apron pass-throughs are strengthened by application of two small sixteen-gauge (1.3 cm) squares on the back of the apron. The blade and apron are scratch brushed and the handle rods are randomly sharp brushed.

This piece is an attractive illustration of minimalism in design. Justine takes her influence and inspiration from her love of Scandinavian design and style and the Bauhaus, which results in objects that are concerned with balance, light, proportion and scale. Her server seems to combine simple Eastern form, in the chopstick-like handle, with a love of geometric shapes and revealed construction.

Artist's philosophy/statement: "I was drawn to working in silver for its inherent qualities: play of light, malleability and a purity that lends itself to clean lines and simple, elegant designs. Silver is for me peaceful to the eye. The cost of silver encourages streamlined, functional design. This is as true for one-off pieces as it is for limited editions. These practical concerns work hand-in-hand with the influences of Modern Movement architecture and Scandinavian design and culture. I try to utilize the virtues of balance, light, rhythm and structure in my work. I want the function of a piece to be immediately apparent, but I strive to make functional objects which nevertheless have the strengths and merits of sculpture. Through experimenting with disc and linear formations, proportion and scale, it became apparent to me that the cake server would retain the characteristics of purity and elegance, also incorporating my own personal philosophies. The techniques that I used had to be as seriously considered as the design, in order to retain purity and elegance. In achieving a clean and minimalistic blade, in producing the cutting edge, I emphasized its form. In consideration of the dual handles, and their weight and construction, I utilized the tension created to incorporate a distinctive feature, highlighted by using an 18k gold rivet. A matte finish enhanced the overall form of the server."

Born: Swindon, Wiltshire, 1971

Training and work: Northbrook College of Design and Technology, 1988–90; BTech National Diploma in Art and Design; Camberwell School of Art, BA (Hons.), 1990–93; extended study, 1993–94; Middlesex University, computer-aided design, 1993; City University Business School, creative business for silversmiths, 1994; workshop studies, 1992; assistant to Simone ten Hompel, 1993; independent work studio, 1994, where she produces a range of tablewares and accessories in the form of one-offs and short-run limited editions.

Goldsmiths' Company Silverware Award, 1993; Goldsmiths' Company winning design, Table Silver Competition, 1994. Various group exhibitions at Business Design Centre; Camberwell School of Art; Turtle Key Arts Centre, Fulham; Buckinghamshire College and elsewhere.

I first learned of Justine's prize-winning work through Rosemary Ransome Wallis. Justine was soon to make the switch from Worthing to London to carry on her early work. She was pleased to have the commission and I was delighted to engage this new young talent in October 1994. After our initial meeting, a flow of telephone and mail correspondence ensued, with a variety of design options to choose from.

Kay Ivanovic

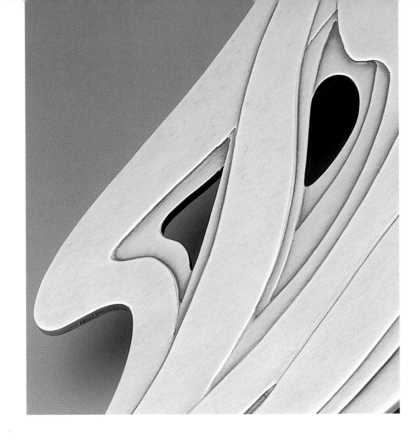

The pierced blade has a fluid scimitar shape reminiscent of later nineteenth-century American wares. It has a single forward positive cusp and sloped rear edge. It is etched into four layers in a flowing pattern over the whole surface. The highly original, parallel split-ribbons lift rises, turns and transforms into a contoured, tubular, tapering handle that is etched over its whole surface in a complementary pattern. The handle is open at both extremities. The surface of the server is lightly anodized and has a lightly brushed satin finish. It will obviously do as well for cake as for fish, and illustrates well the sometimes artificial and semantic nature of the appellations that are used.

This is one of a few servers (see Farrell) with a blade shape that corresponds to a contemporary rendering of the classic scimitar shape. The handle and blade have a rare unity. Here is an object that is returning to a liquid form. The artist has captured and cooled the fluidity of molten metal, transforming it into a cascade of water. The handle swirls with a memory of Art Nouveau, plunging down into the layered depths of the pool below. This is a wonderfully evocative piece, while retaining an acute respect for function, with its graspable handle and generous broad blade.

Artist's philosophy/statement: "Soft sculptural forms are sympathetically overlaid with etched and chased surface decoration inspired by rhythmic patterns in nature."

Born: Philadelphia, USA, 1943
Training and work: Moore College of Art, Philadelphia, BA in illustration, 1967; Sir John Cass School of Art, diploma in silversmithing (with distinction), 1993. Works freelance, mainly to commission. Co-organizer, *Silver to Dine For*, London 1996 and 1998.

Commendation, Goldsmiths' Company Craftsman of the Year, 1979; first runner-up, Goddard's Silver Awards, 1981; first prize, designer silver, Goldsmiths' Company Craftsman of the Year, 1986; winner, The Silver Trust plate competition, 1990. Exhibited *Loot, Superloot* 1979, 1981; Goldsmiths' Fair, 1984, 1986–87, 1989–90; *Craft of the Silversmith*, Grey Harris, Bristol, 1988; Chelsea, California, 1990; *Trompe l'Oeil*, Connoisseur Gallery, 1996; Napkin Ring collection, Goldsmiths' Hall, 1996; *Silver to Dine For*, London, 1996. Commissioned work in St John's College, Cambridge, The Silver Trust 10 Downing Street Collection and private collections.

I first saw Kay's work at a display of silversmith's work at the Chelsea Crafts Fair, London, in 1996. A wonderful etched beaker caught my attention. I undertook to meet Kay shortly thereafter in order to learn more of her background and work. She has trained in both the USA and the UK and has developed her own mode of work.

Fish slice

Sterling silver

London 1997

Length 14 in. (35.5 cm)

Weight 13.3 oz (413 g)

Rod Kelly

A touch of gold, whether more or less, is a Kelly trademark. The textured forged trowel blade is pointed and has sharply turned shoulders on a generally rounded contour. The blade is one of only a very few slices that is domed, rather than being flat or dished. It is dramatically chased with a sensuous enveloping fish (trout) that rides on the pierced swirling foam. The hollow-box handle, made in nine pieces, rises on an angular vertical lift construction and shows a fish half-buried in the rippling sea.

This server refers back to the Rococo style of the mid-eighteenth century, but gives it a new interpretation, revealing a wonderful mastery of chasing decoration. Kelly's hallmark is his exquisite low-relief chasing, and the way that he creates a linear, flowing narrative. He feels very much a part of the Arts and Crafts tradition, designing the integral form and decoration, raising or making the piece, and executing the decoration. His luxuriant chasing is always controlled within borders and clearly delineated spaces; it is at once exuberant and restrained. His work is as much about pattern as about texture. He eschews a highly polished surface in favour of revealed hammer marks, another connection with the Arts and Crafts Movement. Arthur Grimwade has expressed his amazement at Kelly's "fluidity of handling and aesthetics. We talk about shape but not enough about the aesthetics of silver."[18]

Artist's philosophy/statement: Kelly's pieces "are functional, creative and well-crafted. His designs are based on the flowing lines of natural forms."[19] He states: "The blade has a curved Gothic outline … As chasing is a technique of depth and layers, I thought it strange to [pierce] the background, as this might take away the effect of the deepest layers. … When the chasing was complete it immediately made sense of the design and the function of the fish slice." He goes on to say: "I take pride in the relationship between myself and the person commissioning a work and gain a great deal of satisfaction from it. I enjoy talking through the design and the making of a piece and, at a later stage, inviting the person to my workshop to see the work in progress. I particularly like meeting clients in their homes; it is one of the greatest pleasures of commissioned work and I've met some very interesting people."[20]

Born: Reading, Berkshire, 1956

Training and work: Preston Polytechnic, foundation course, 1975; Birmingham Polytechnic, first class (Hons.) 3-D design, 1979; Royal College of Art, 1983, under Gerald Benney. Occasional teaching, including polytechnics of Leicester, Lancashire, Birmingham and Manchester; visiting professor at Bishopsland (P&O Makower Trust). He established his own workshop in 1984. He serves on a number of professional councils.

Freeman of the Goldsmiths' Company, 1985. Numerous special exhibitions, prizes and awards, including first prize, 'Excellence Awards' Trophies, McVitie Company; first prize, Goddard's Silver Awards, 1983; Craftsman of the Year, senior group, Goldsmiths' Hall; *Rising Stars* exhibition, Goldsmiths' Hall, 1990. Many important commissions for royalty, museums, churches and public bodies, including Lichfield Cathedral Collection and The Silver Trust 10 Downing Street Collection; many national and international exhibitions at galleries, museums and institutions.

I first encountered Rod in 1988, just as his career was about to experience a meteoric rise. I saw a display of his chasing at the Design Fair of the Worshipful Company of Goldsmiths in London. His exposition and deep motivation led to a first commission for a stunning 'egret' beaker – an overall design of a bird in a field of rushes. Kelly now pursues his work in Norfolk, where he lives with his wife, Sheila McDonald, herself a well-known enameller, and their children. Kelly shares Gerald Benney's concern for the state and preservation of the craft. He fears that techniques such as chasing and its lore might be lost. His was my first commission.

Fish slice

Sterling silver, save for a golden fish-eye

London 1989

Length 13 ⅜ in (34 cm)

Weight 10.5 oz (326 g)

Rod Kelly

Cake/pie slice
Sterling silver with gold
London 1997
Length 14 ½ in. (37 cm)
Weight 10 oz (311 g)

This second piece by Kelly was stimulated, in part, by the exhibition of the collection at Goldsmiths' Hall, London, in 1995. He offered to make a cake server with a somewhat freer feeling than his elegant fish slice. His choice of 'cake' also had a personal motivation, which is revealed below. His essay that follows describes the piece and sheds light on the nature and problems of silverwork design:

I initially produced a design that would convey the low-relief chasing and be a very elegant form. Some months later, when I commenced work on the piece, I felt that I would like to change the handle: the one I had designed was too pedestrian, too functional, and did not evoke any humour, subtlety or originality. Normally, when first starting a design, I would draw with a pencil, freehand, the shape of an object; I would then work out (if there were several curves involved) where the centres lie. I would then re-draw the object, using a compass to outline the curves, in this case the blade of the cake slice. I usually find that the distance and proportion of the radii and the distance between compass points, along with the general measurements of the object, have a fixed relationship. If this is calculated as a proportion I then use the ratio as closely as possible to construct the rest of the piece, *i.e.* the handle.

The blade takes the shape of a Gothic arch with a curved side at the back of the blade. It has a ridge running along the centre; this is in common with several other recent pieces that have been scored and folded. Normally a blade is flat but in this case the ridge creates two sides so that one side of the chasing will always be in shadow. This adds to the depth of the chasing. I liked the irony that a cake slice should be flat. In this case, the pie or cake would be cut with one of the sides of the blade; the slice could then be inverted and used as a scoop or serving trowel. The shape of the inverted blade would help contain the piece. The ridge was to extend right through the form along the blade and continue along the handle; this gives the end of the handle, where it meets the blade, more visual weight.

I wanted the theme of the slice decoration to be evocative of my childhood, of seeing my mother make cakes and pies. I have represented the pie-crust pattern on the side of the slide. The blackberries and bramble leaves are chased in low relief in a swirling pattern. The thorns are inlaid with fine gold. This involves carving out the shape with engraving tools, down to half of the depth of the metal; the sides of the shape are then undercut with a chisel. A piece of fine gold is then cut to shape and dropped into the detail that had been carved out. When the gold is planished, it spreads under the undercut and is held in place. The inlaid gold details start on the left of the blade and form a swirling pattern along the decoration to the point of the blade, where there is also an inlaid detail.

The handle joins the blade by way of a shaped, shallow, hollow form that is reminiscent of a blackberry seed; there are other very small seeds in the details on the chased blade. The round endpiece of the handle is also chased with blackberry detail and a small leaf pattern. The handle itself is chased with a pattern of thorns and has a full curved underbelly. When positioned on the table I wanted the end of the handle to touch the surface. At the rounded end of the handle, the slice is engraved on the underside in single-line letters: *For My Mother A.J.K.*

Chris Knight

This is a trowel, with unusual blade shape and handle. The heavy asymmetric blade is bevelled on both edges and spreads to the left. It has a fuzzy 'stainless steel pad' swirled finish. It is made from twelve-gauge (2 mm) sheet. The bold, strong, polished lift-piece comes forward on the top of the blade in a short rat-tail; it holds the cone-shaped handle firmly in an embracing ring-and-screw arrangement. The handle has a whitened finish and carries a series of short truncated spikes over its surface.

Spiked forms, highly polished cones and knobs, and a preoccupation with poise and balance have been the defining characteristics of Knight's exploration of silver hollow-ware. For this server he has also explored the contrast between the polished blade and the matte handle. Knight sends a message in much of his works: Life is thorny but make the most of it. In this case the knobbed handle proves quite comfortable and firm to the grasp. The artist skilfully combines his message with function because he is interested in form and function above the decorative symbolism of association.

Artist's philosophy/statement: "The object should express itself and not a related subject. It should exist and be celebrated in its own right. The handle should be exulted for the way it is held and the slice should be enjoyed in the way it serves ... but that solution will be in conflict with other and essential instincts if it does not at the same time provide an aesthetic solution. ... I could not design a fish slice that was merely a trowel, that ... could just as easily have been used by a brick-layer. ... With these thoughts in mind I proceeded with the design, starting with references drawn from machine tools and Japanese kitchen knives and developing form through practical tests. Ultimately the utensil has to be fit for its purpose ... These practical qualities would not necessarily be basic but [would be] enhanced to create a bolder expression ..."[22]

Born: Bishop's Stortford, Hertfordshire, 1964

Training and work: Harlow Technical College, Essex, art and design, 1983–84; Sheffield City Polytechnic, 3-D design in silversmithing and jewellery, BA (Hons.) first class, 1984–87; Royal College of Art, metalwork and jewellery, 1990–92. Designer, Derick Simpson Goldsmiths, New Haven, 1988–90; Chris Knight Design, Sheffield, 1992– ; visiting lecturer, Sheffield Hallam University, 1992– ; lecturer, Liverpool Hope University College, 1993– . Founder-member, Association of British Designer Silversmiths.

Runner-up, Platinum Awards, 1985–86; runner-up, Canning Bicentenary Award, 1986–87; Sheffield Assay Office Award, 1987; Guardians Standard of Wrought Plate Award, 1987; winner, Levi's Design Competition, 1991; Royal College of Art, B. Yehia Prize, 1992; Crafts Council Award, 1993; London Arts Board grant, 1993; New Exhibitors' prize, Chelsea Crafts Fair, 1993; Liverpool Hope University research grant, 1995; Yorkshire and Humberside Artists' Award, 1996. Many solo and group exhibitions at Goldsmiths' Hall, Royal College of Art, Crafts Council, The Scottish Gallery and other venues in UK, USA and Belgium. Commissions for the Crafts Council, Goldsmiths' Company, P&O Makower Trust, Sheffield Hallam University and the Sheffield Public Art Commission. His work has been the subject of comment and description in many crafts publications and reviews.[21]

Chris and I met in October 1996 at the Chelsea Crafts Fair. I had previously seen a number of examples of his work on display at several sites in London. Over a cup of coffee I had a profitable discussion with him about a research paper on art and style that he had written for his Master's degree, and that had been sent to me earlier by Helen Clifford.

Server

Sterling silver

Sheffield 1997

Length 12 ⅝ in. (32 cm)

Weight 14.7 oz (457 g)

Cake slice
Sterling silver
Edinburgh 1992
Length 14 ½ in. (36.7 cm)
Weight 14.5 oz (450 g)

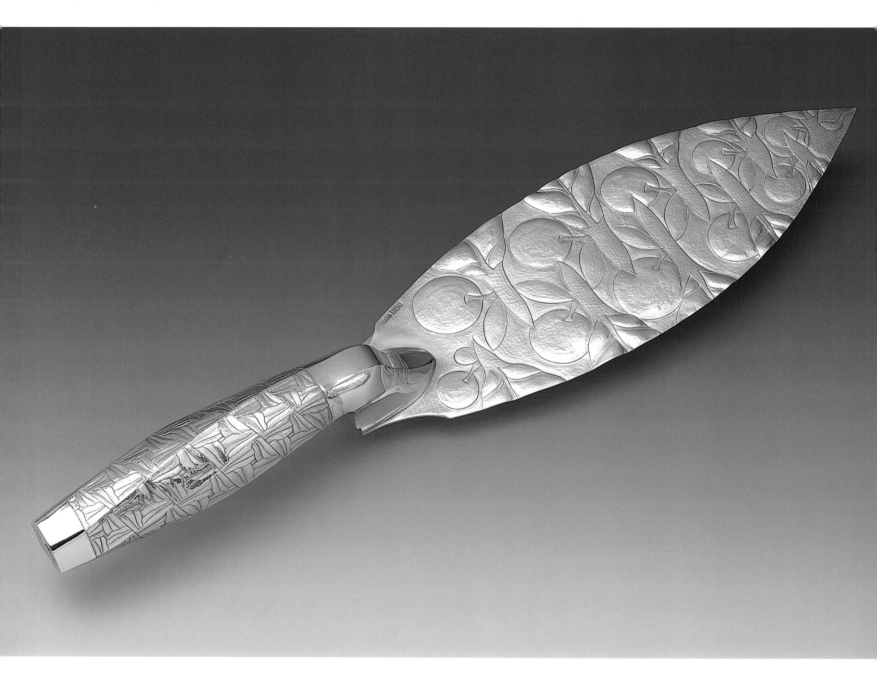

Michael Lloyd

The blade is a symmetrical, long, oval, near-navette shape. The sheet blade is unpierced and completely chased to the edges with apples, part leaves, and leaf stems ending in points. The handle is chased with repeated rectangles of four intersecting leaf parts set in file on six swirled linear panels. The handle has a polished endpiece and a five-faceted heavy boss that is integrated with the faceted rising lift. The butt of the handle is chased with four intersecting part apples. Lloyd is a skilled silversmith and does his own raising and forging.

Lloyd is especially distinguished for his beautiful flat chasing of themes from nature. He draws directly from life and "is able to distil the essence of a form; the clarity and rhythm of his emotive images … and strong simple forms produce pieces of quiet harmony which are … timeless".[23] This server reflects the long oval shape of two hundred years ago; but unlike those, the filled handles of which lie in the plane of the blade (fig. 4, p. 14), the artist has continued the apple theme of the blade on to the very substantial handle that lifts from the blade. Even the butt end is exquisitely finished – although, alas, not visible in the illustration. Lloyd has carried the chasing right to the edge of the blade, as he has frequently done on the rims of beakers and cups: he explains that "Nature is ongoing; it is not appro-

priate to break it off prematurely". He bears witness to the philosophy of the Arts and Crafts Movement.

Artist's philosophy/statement: "In looking for justifications and motivation for work, the word 'homage' sings out, not only for the beauty of life and landscape but also for our own creativity. I hope my work reflects my deep love of nature. It is a celebration of our surrounding and (I hope) the work will have some spirit of healing – we create our own environment, sometimes to the detriment of humanity, and sometimes lifting … for me, the objective of work becomes a spiritual act, an act of thanksgiving … "[24]

Born: Salisbury, Wiltshire, 1950

Training and work: School of Silversmithing, Birmingham, under Ralph Baxendale and Derick Birch, first class (Hons.), 1973; Royal College of Art, under Gerald Benney and Robert Goodden, 1976. In the period 1976–89 he set up a workshop and small school aboard the Dutch barge *Spaarnestroom*, travelling and working in Holland, Belgium and France. In 1989 he returned to the Galloway coast and set up a studio with emphasis on ecclesiastical work. He specializes in chasing and hand-raised silver. The rural setting of his home and workshop is integral to his work.

During his period of travel, Lloyd was awarded the John Player and *Telegraph* Craftsman of the Year and the *Gesellschaft für Goldschmiedekunst Laurells* – the top awards for chasing. He received a Scottish Development Agency fellowship in 1991. He is a Freeman of the Goldsmiths' Company. Lloyd's creations are represented by many commissions for royalty and government, and for churches and cathedrals throughout England, including the Lichfield Cathedral Collection. His work is in the Victoria and Albert Museum, Goldsmiths' Hall, Crafts Council Collection, Royal Scottish Museum, Fitzwilliam Museum, Lincolnshire Museum, Lloyd's Insurance, St John's College, Cambridge, The Royal Society, The Silver Trust 10 Downing Street Collection and elsewhere. In 1999 he was commissioned to make the mace for the Scottish Assembly. He has exhibited widely.

Michael and I met in the autumn of 1991 at my flat in London. It was such a pleasure to meet this informal, charming, unpretentious person who lives his sentiments about life. As with several other commissions, I simply suggested he get on with it and surprise me with the result.

Server

Blade of sterling silver, the handle of sterling
and silver/copper *mokumé* and 14k gold

London 1992

Length 15 ½ in. (39.5 cm)

Total weight 15.5 oz (481 g)

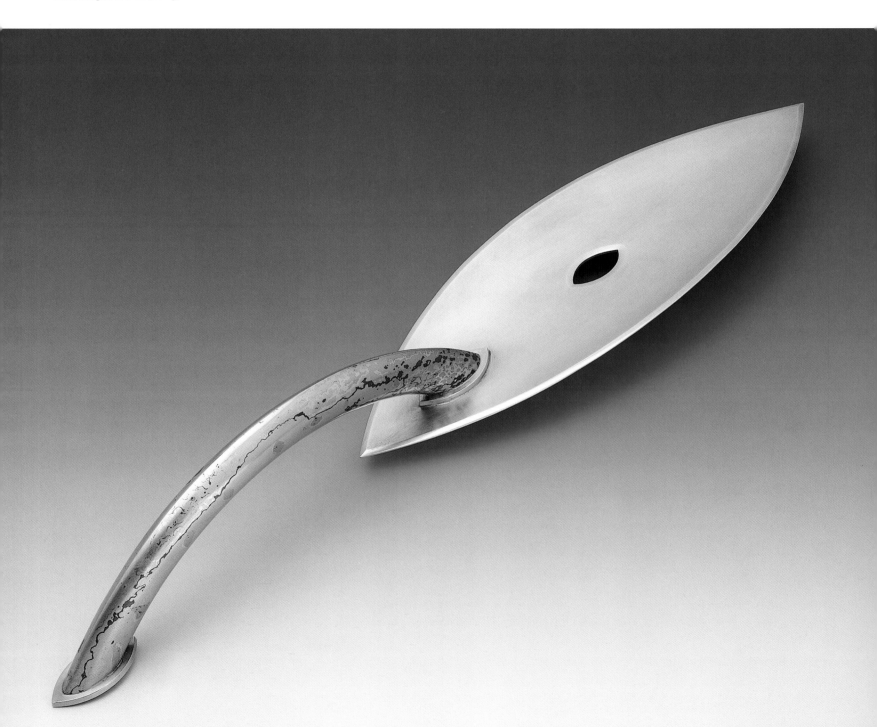

Alistair McCallum

The blade is a simple, undecorated, forged, long, oval, navette shape with a matte finish, and is centrally pierced with a shape that echoes the blade. The latter is slightly dished along the long axis and is bevelled on all edges. The handle is a solid symmetric arc of elliptic cross-section, having a silver/copper *mokumé* surface that appears as seaweed decoration. The handle attaches to the blade with a navette-shaped gold boss and has the same-style finial. Although identified as a fish server, the article is as well adapted for cake and other service.

The maker's play on symmetry – with complementary and opposed arcs between blade and handle – shows his well-founded sense of design. McCallum has a great sense of minimal form that is almost as Oriental as the *mokumé gané* technique that he has made his own. What is not there is as important as what is included; curve balances curve, shapes are repeated, echoed, balanced, positive space plays with negative space, light with shadow. In this way a tremendous harmony and tranquillity are created – a type of visual and formal poetry. Function and proportion are integral to the total concept. With only modest and unstressed surface decoration of the handle, the piece nevertheless makes a strong statement: handle and blade work together from tip to tip as one – and not as two separate, conjoined pieces.

Artist's philosophy/statement: "I trained as a jeweller interested in bringing colour and contrast to the work by combining different materials. This led … eventually to the Japanese technique of *mokumé gané* … I was drawn to increase the scale which led to producing vessels and containers. This meant concerning myself with silversmithing techniques. … Owing to the highly decorative nature of *mokumé*, I have always believed that this necessitates simplicity of form." With regard to this commission, "One of my main aims was to find a simple and effective shape that would work in both aesthetic and functional terms. I wanted to avoid an over-embellished and fussy object. … I decided that I would base the design on curves and ovaloid shapes. The only decoration would be contrast between metals. … I made the handle from silver and copper *mokumé gané*. The blade is of silver and, to add a richness of colour, 14k gold was used for the end [plates] of the handle."

Born: Middlesbrough, Cleveland, 1953

Training and work: Teesside College of Art, foundation studies, 1972; Loughborough College of Art, BA silversmithing and jewellery, 1975; Royal College of Art, 1978. Part-time lecturer, Middlesex Polytechnic and Camberwell College of Art. He has made a special study of *mokumé gané*, a traditional Japanese metalworking technique.

Royal College of Art, travel award to Japan, 1978; Goldsmiths' Company, Littledale award, 1979; Crafts Council, new craftsman grant, 1979; Camberwell School of Art, research grant, 1979; Sotheby's, decorative arts award exhibition, London and Japan, 1988. Work in collections of Victoria and Albert Museum, Crafts Council, Goldsmiths' Company, Royal Museum of Scotland, Leeds Art Galleries, Art Gallery of Western Australia and others. Numerous group and solo exhibitions in UK, Germany, Switzerland, Belgium, Holland, France, USA, Australia and Japan.

Alistair and I first met in 1991 at a Goldsmiths' Fair at the Hall, where his beautiful mokumé gané *work, about which I had already heard, came to my attention. His cheerful, pleasant demeanour prompted a long conversation. A commission followed a visit to Alistair's home workshop in Lewisham, south London. He has been a leader in the use of mixed metals in England. Alistair is one of a remarkable complement of talented smiths who have been associated with the Camberwell College of Art.*

Michael McCrory

Cake slice/lifter
Sterling silver
London 1998
Length (without handle) 9 ¼ in. (23.5 cm)
Weight 12.8 oz (399 g)

The lyre-shaped blade is sharpened on the ends and the blade halves are strengthened by a sub-surface join towards the front end. The blade carries a simple decorative design of pierced holes that outlines its inner division. An anticlastic hollow handle, 8 in. (20.5 cm) long, rises up at an acute angle at the rear. It curls forward so that the hand is over the blade, the long extent of which provides a considerable useful surface.

This server encapsulates the principles of elegance through simplicity, of form and decoration. The blade celebrates the high polish that silver takes, while its satisfyingly solid mass is rendered light through the central opening and twenty-one drilled decorative holes. The sense of delicacy combined with strength is carried up into the arched handle, which echoes the curvaceous lines of the blade. McCrory has achieved a harmony of form and function, sculptural presence and line.

Artist's philosophy/statement: "Silverware to me has to be aesthetically pleasing with a sculptural visual strength. My designs are founded on balance of line, form and proportion, which harmonize with the detail in the tactile finished form."

Born: Northern Ireland, 1943

Training and work: Belfast College of Art, silversmithing diploma, 1961–65; Sir John Cass School of Art, postgraduate, 1965–67; National Diploma in design-silversmithing. Lecturer, Belfast College of Art, 1967–70; senior lecturer, 1970–90, and head, 1990–96, School of Fine and Applied Arts, University of Ulster. Freelance silversmithing, 1996– . Committee member, Guild of Designer Craftsmen of Northern Ireland, 1985–89. Various offices and duties in Crafts Council of Ireland, 1987– , and Arts Council of Northern Ireland, 1989–90. Board member, Craftswork (Northern Ireland), 1989–94.

British Design Award. Many commissions for badges of office, trophies, domestic ware *etc.*, including a mace and two staves for the University of Ulster and the Presidential heraldic shield in Dublin Castle.

Michael and I have never met. I was led to contact him by telephone at his home in County Down after seeing a photograph of his beautiful creation included in the teapot exhibition at Goldsmiths' Hall in June 1998. Several postal and telephone exchanges led to this final, exciting – surprise – design.

Angus McFadyen

The trowel shape has a highly rounded blade made from fourteen-gauge (1.6 mm) sheet. It is highly pierced, with a blackberry bramble leaf, vine and thorn motif. The whole surface is finely line engraved – vines, leaves and thorns – and the leaves are gilded on both top and bottom surfaces; the latter is also engraved with the outline of the top-side pattern. The hollow handle is made in four pieces. It rises from the blade without intermediate lift. It has an angular cusped shape that echoes the vines and thorns. Its underside is rounded for comfort, the upper surface is plain.

This 'bramble' server is a restatement of the eighteenth-century trowel, which is one of several universal shapes that naturally appear if a server is intended to be functional. Beyond that, however, it owes little to precedent, whether in form or ornament. It springs from nature. Texture and contrast are key features. The angular handle, which abstracts a thorned branch, meets a delicately pierced and intricately engraved blade. The finely delineated thorned twiglets and the gilt leaves of the bramble, with their realistic veins, set off the high polish and form of the handle. The decorative nature of the blade recalls the sensitivity of the Arts and Crafts Movement to natural form and its stylization.

Artist's philosophy/statement: "My interest in silversmithing stems largely from an enjoyment of using traditional methods of working metal. In the past two or three years I have become very interested in engraving. These are techniques I have learned because I like … hand engraving. I find the tools and their use as appealing as the effect they achieve. Beginning to engrave a piece of silver has the same thrill as beginning a drawing on a clean sheet of paper."

Born: Bristol, 1962

Training and work: Bristol Polytechnic, foundation course, 1980–81; Manchester Polytechnic, 3-D design, BA (Hons.), 1981–84. Lecturer, Wrexham College of Art and Design, 1987–89; Manchester Polytechnic, 1989. Consultant in India for Indian Trade Mission to the EEC, 1990. Independent studio, 1984– . Manchester Metropolitan University, candidate, PhD programme, 3-D design 1994– .

Regular exhibitor with *Dazzle*, London, Manchester, Edinburgh and Glasgow. Goldsmiths' Fair, London, 1986–96, and Chelsea Crafts Fair; exhibitions in Edinburgh.

I first encountered Angus's work at one of the annual Goldsmiths' Fairs organized each October to expose the work of silversmiths to the public. His original and unique style made his creations stand out. Unfortunately, I had to wait a year, until the next fair, before I could ask him to make a server, but we were then in immediate agreement on the whole enterprise.

Cake slice

Sterling silver, partial gilt

Edinburgh 1996

Length 12 in. (30.5 cm)

Weight 5.7 oz (177 g)

Cake/pie slice

Sterling silver, enamel

London 1995

Length 12 5/8 in. (32 cm)

Weight 13.6 oz (422 g)

Enamelled finial by Frances Loyen

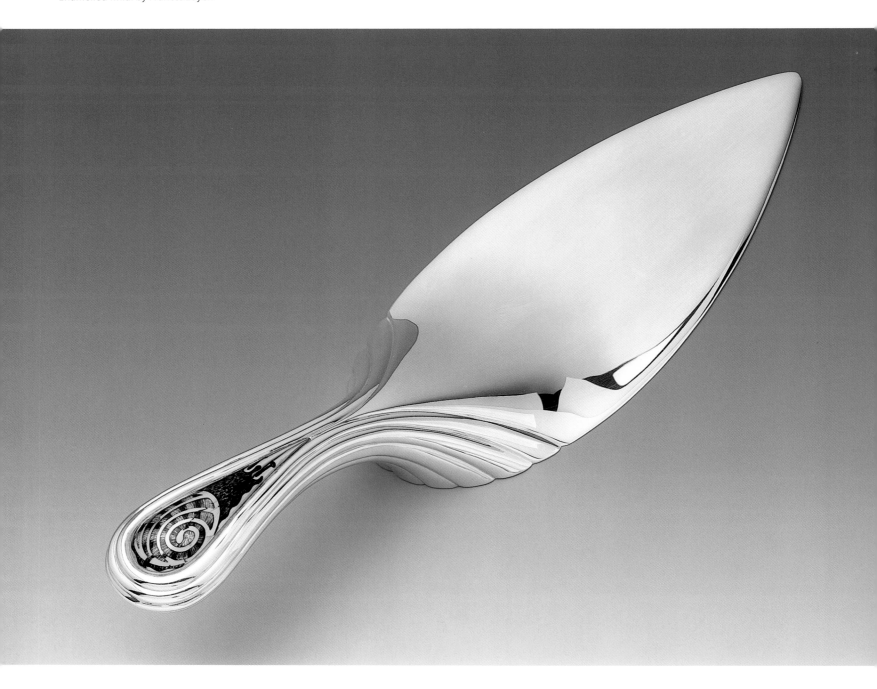

Hector Miller

The blade is an elongated trowel form from which the handle continues, ostensibly in one piece. The handle and blade are actually invisibly welded in several parts; inaccessible seams are masked by a concave soldered under-heel piece. The handle rises from a waisted stem, which is conveyed by a multi-fluted array that first narrows and then widens to circumscribe and embrace an enamelled finial. The enamelling is a partially gilt, blue-grey snail. The surfaces of the blade and handle are highly polished.

This slice bear's Miller's tell-tale signature, a smooth finish highlighted by a keen sense of decorative detail. The integral nature of blade and handle is reinforced by the dynamic fluting, which gives this slice a sense of movement, reminiscent of the 'speed whiskers' of 1930s design. This is tied to the decorative flourish of the enamel, which focuses the eyes and provides texture and depth.

Artist's philosophy/statement: "My primary concerns when designing a piece of silver are always with form, proportion, detailing and practicality. As a craftsman, this creative process is tempered by my working knowledge of the materials used and the techniques available for shaping them to the highest standards. I enjoy the challenge of creating new manufacturing systems: for instance, adapting steel-welding equipment for joining silver without a visible seam. I often derive design ideas from such inventive workshop methods; for me, art and science are indivisible."[25]

Born: Rusper, West Sussex, 1945

Training and work: Hornsey College of Art, silversmithing and jewellery, 1965–68; Royal College of Art under Professor Gooden, MDes, 1971. Freelance and designer/manager with Stuart Devlin, 1972–74. Established own company, 1974– .

Liveryman of the Goldsmiths' Company, 1986. Numerous exhibitions at Goldsmiths' Hall, from 1968 to present. Exhibitions in Switzerland, Belgium and elsewhere, including the Hallmark Silver Collection. Numerous commissions, including British Commonwealth Games, English cathedrals, Shah of Iran, Royal Yacht Squadron, Old Kirk, Edinburgh, Vintners' Company, Goldsmiths' Company, The Silver Trust 10 Downing Street Collection and others.

Hector holds the record for time elapsed between commissioning, in 1994, and delivery, in 1998. The long interval has occasioned the lovely enamelled finial décor by Frances Loyen, and the name he gave the server – the "snail slice". We concluded our agreement at his workshop in Kentish Town, London, which he took over from Leslie Durbin (q.v.). The delay was caused by Hector's great success in industrial design. The blade was assayed in 1995 and the whole assembled in 1998. When I went to his workshop Hector gave me an exposition of his various enterprises, as well as a demonstration of his new technique of silver welding. Very exciting to a novice silversmith!

Fish slice

Sterling silver, moonstone

London 1999

Length 9⅝ in. (24.5 cm)

Weight 10.9 oz (340 g)

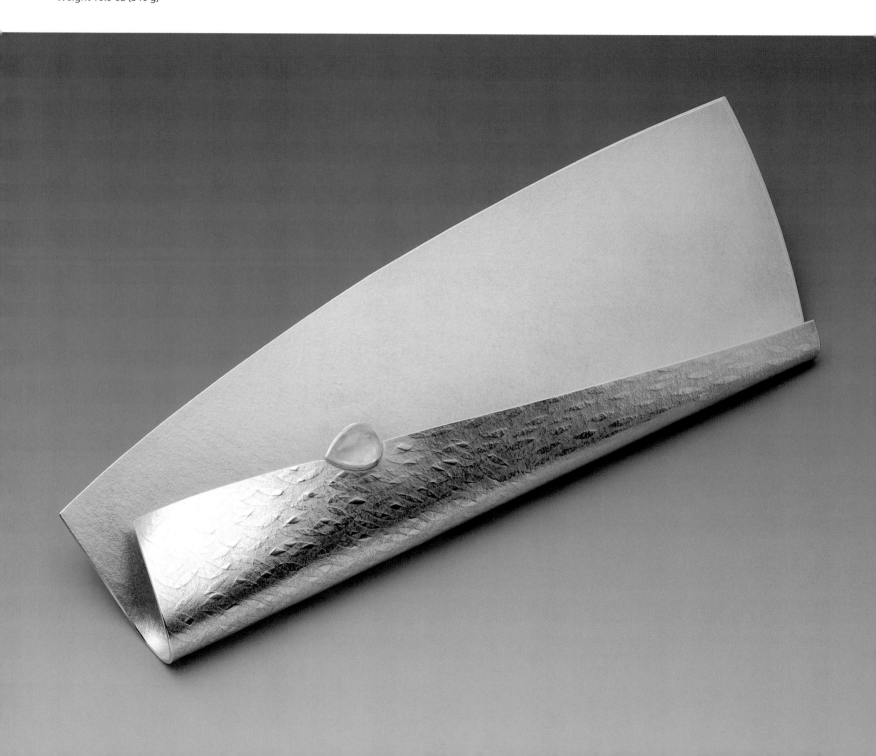

Jacqueline Mina

The server is fabricated from a contoured quadrilateral silver sheet. An under-edge area is cross-roller printed with a stylized shoal of fish that displays matte and shiny detail. This patterned part is rolled over so as to fashion a scoop with a bevelled leading edge. Interesting contrast is provided between the patterned surface and the finely hammered surface underneath. A drop-shaped moonstone is applied to the upper edge.

The innovative design of this server stems from the fertile imagination of a jeweller. Unencumbered by the long tradition of silver flatware, Mina has approached the brief from a refreshingly new perspective. The elegant simplicity of a folded sheet forms both functional blade and useful handle. Although the design solution is excitingly simple, the attention to detail in texture and finish make it a gorgeously rich sculptural piece. The roll of the silver captures the motion of a wave, where silky smooth depths are contrasted by the pattern of the surface spray. The single moonstone focuses the eye and evokes the iridescence of fish scales and the glint of sun on sea.

Artist's philosophy/statement: "In my work I aim to achieve an aesthetic result which obscures the technical rigours of its production. I am preoccupied mainly with the surfaces of precious metals (which I always affect in some way before construction begins) and with form – juxtaposing the play of light, reflection, lustre with characteristic angle, curve and line – inspired by an abstraction of Nature, particularly the human form. Observation of the body, through dance and life drawing, has always been central to my visual language. I am intrigued, too, by the potential for dialogue between inner and outer planes, with random patterns imprisoned within strictly delineated edges and the visual tension created by the contrast and harmony of all these factors."

Born: Buckinghamshire, 1942

Training and work: Hornsey College of Arts and Crafts, silversmithing and embroidery, 1957–62; Royal College of Art, jewellery, 1962–65. Part-time teaching, including: Harrow School of Art; West Surrey College of Art; St Mary's College, Strawberry Hill; Leicester Polytechnic; Epsom School of Art; Sir John Cass School of Art; Middlesex Polytechnic. Visiting lecturer, Royal College of Art, 1972–94. Service on various professional committees.

Liveryman of the Goldsmiths' Company, 1995. First prize, De Beers ring competition, 1968. Numerous important commissions, including: De Beers Ladies Race, Ascot, and George VI and Elizabeth II Diamond Stakes, Ascot; Victoria and Albert Museum; Ayrton Metals; Goldsmiths' Company. Collections of Crafts Council; Leeds City Art Galleries; Victoria and Albert Museum; Royal Scottish Museum; Cooper-Hewitt Museum, New York. Many solo and group exhibitions, both British and international. Her jewellery work is the subject of dozens of books, magazine articles, catalogues and radio and television features.[26]

Jacqueline and I first met in 1995 at Goldsmiths' Hall and, thereafter, on a number of occasions at various exhibitions and openings. My admiration for her work led to a very early invitation to make a piece for the collection, which was politely sidetracked owing to her other commitments. In 1998, however, she finally acceded.

Peter Musgrove

This piece has a flat, polished, spade-shaped blade. This is pierced with seven rows of fish, depicted in outline and held in a minimal curvilinear net that was engraved by Malcolm Appleby (q.v.). The round tapering rod handle is novel in its orientation – curving back towards the blade. It is completely chased with beautiful scalework and terminates in a ball drop. It attaches underneath the rear of the blade, which is raised in a hemispherical cone shape to receive the handle, which is flattened underside into the plane of the blade. Despite its weight, the server is excellently balanced and surprisingly light in the hand.

This server is of a novel flat-iron construction that is simple, functional, and elegant in its conception. It mingles the antique and the modern. The regimented ranks of the shoal of fish with which the trowel-like blade has been pierced are held together by engraved serpentine curves that suggest their watery environment, and reflect the overall shape of the blade. The scrolling is echoed in the arch of the scaled handle, which unites the flat plane of the blade with the three-dimensional writhe of the tail, integrating the form and ornament. This server is visually and physically satisfying in its balance, proportion and unity. Although undeniably contemporary, it incorporates references to late eighteenth-century serpent handles, to the traditional trowel blade, and to the early eighteenth-century love of the Rococo scroll.

Artist's philosophy/statement: "I have many happy memories of the server, as with all my favourite pieces. Although technically challenging, they create and almost make themselves."

Born: London, 1946

Training and work: Central School of Art, pre-apprenticeship, 1962, followed by a traditional silversmith apprenticeship at C.J. Vander Ltd, 1963–67; Hornsey College of Art, diploma course, 1967–70; worked with the noted architect/silversmith Louis Osman, 1970–72. Established independent workshop, 1972. Outwork for Louis Osman and Malcolm Appleby. For the past several years he has also been technician-lecturer at the Royal College of Art.

First prize and medallist, City Guilds Technological examination. Many important commissions for livery companies, including: Wax Chandlers; Ironmongers and Curriers; also a Warden's cup for the Goldsmiths' Company and a Prime Warden's cup for the Architects' Company; a large dish and jugs for the University of East Anglia; and three ciboria for Norwich Cathedral.

Following a telephone conversation, I met Peter at our flat in London. After I received the slice from Malcolm Appleby, the carcase of which was made by Peter, I determined to have a piece by him. Peter's contribution became one of a unique pair: the slice he made, carrying his mark and engraved by Malcolm Appleby, and Malcolm's slice, engraved by him and carrying his mark, but with the carcase made by Peter.

Fish slice

Sterling silver

London 1992

Length 6 7/8 in. (17.5 cm)

Weight 20.3 oz (630 g)

Engraving by Malcolm Appleby

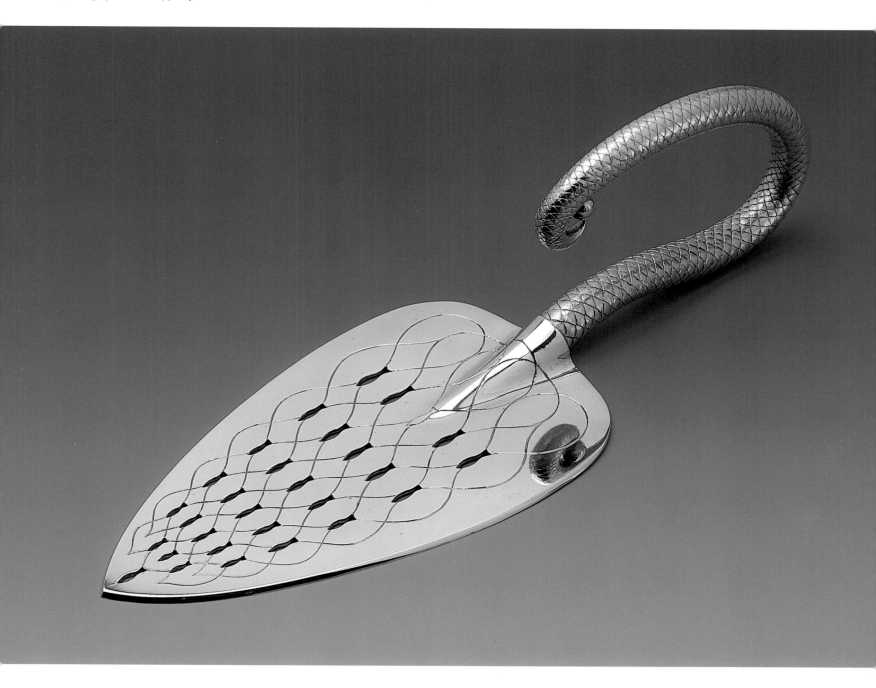

Fish slice

Sterling silver

London 1998

Length 15 in. (38 cm)

Weight 14.3 oz (446 g)

Shannon O'Neill

The blade has a rounded oval trowel shape and is unique in being of hollow construction. The bottom surface is flat; the top surface is domed and is beautifully chased in an asymmetric eddy swirl, from the vortex of which a fish body, with fluted tail, emerges. The handle is also hollow and made in three sections. It has a matte finish, in contrast with the polished blade.

Although the relationship between silver and ceramics has a long and distinguished history – via the work of such designers as Nicholas Sprimont in the eighteenth century – more recent connections between these materials have been rare. O'Neill, who first trained in ceramics, approaches silver with a modeller's skill, exploiting the plasticity of the metal with a sculptor's confidence. O'Neill created a maquette in plaster to put form to her ideas before working with the metal. The sensuous curve of the fleshy tail that forms the handle rises up and out of the deeply fluted trowel, creating an organic unity of function and sculpture.

Artist's philosophy/statement: "My love of dance, training in ceramics, and childhood spent growing up by the ocean has inspired me to design and create flowing, graceful and powerful pieces of silver tableware. Poise, stance, movement and momentum are all integral ingredients in a dancer's training, which I have carried through into my silversmithing. Each piece of tableware that I design or create attempts to capture the grace and beauty of a dancer, alongside the rhythm and majesty of the ocean."

Born: Leeds, West Yorkshire, 1971

Training and work: Manchester Metropolitan University, first class in 3-D design BA, 1995. Study at New York State University, scholarship in ceramics; also University of New Delhi, sculpture. Worked on design and construction of puppets for children's television and films, Cosgrove Hall Productions and various US advertising agencies, including Warner Brothers. Training at Nayler Brothers workshop, London, 1995.

Young Designer Silversmith of the Year Award, Goldsmiths' Company, 1996. Exhibited at Victoria and Albert Museum, and Garrard Collections of Manchester City Art Galleries, Yuken (UK) Ltd. Commissions: Manchester Metropolitan University; St Albans Church, Wirral; The Silver Trust 10 Downing Street Collection; and a number of private individuals.

I first learned of Shannon's accomplishments from Rosemary Ransome Wallis. We met in London at the Crafts Council and she agreed to make a server for me. Her painstaking nature occasioned a small delay while she first perfected herself in a technique she intended to employ. She eventually delivered the server to me in Seattle, where she had come to visit friends. Her wonderful maquette in parianware was an inspirational bonus. I enjoyed showing her the University of Washington's fine metal-design facilities, where I had practised the craft on occasion, courtesy of John Marshall (q.v.).

Justin Richardson (and Steven Ottewill)

The blade is derived from the long oval shape and has a bevelled left edge and a wide, scalloped, fin-like, raised right side. The raised handle is of hollow construction and consists of two intertwined rolling curves that splay out into a four-leaf flower holding a lapis lazuli cabochon finial. It has a bright butler finish, contrasted by the ribbed section.

The slice displays a dynamic fluidity that successfully evokes its marine association. Richardson has used a strong outline to suggest the shape of a fish, with a hint of fin and twist of tail to conjure up the essence of 'fishness' without ever becoming literal. The design and skilful workmanship confer on the hard, rigid metal a fluidity that is almost unique in the collection. The fin has a function beyond decoration, as it holds the served contents in place. Asymmetry and regularity meet, as do patterned and plain surface. The use of semiprecious stones – here lapis lazuli – is reminiscent of Arts and Crafts and Art Nouveau work. The deep blue of the lapis serves as a reminder of the blue of the sea.

Artist's philosophy/statement: "In my design I have been influenced by the fluidity of the sea and its inhabitants without employing the literal interpretation. ...

My projects have traditionally been utility led, and within a classical tradition of silverware design ... but I have added other criteria to the creative choice process. I have a profound interest in the artistic movements of the beginning of the twentieth century, and consider a knowledge of that which has gone before an essential springboard for the departure of the new. Some of our greatest influences have been from the Art Nouveau period. Our primary enthusiasm for the timeless forms of natural objects is also echoed in this period. ... A commission for a fish server provides an almost perfect arena for the interplay of such ideas: a practical object brings with it essential criteria for ease of handling and efficient operation – a rigid structure within which the designer must be constrained. There is an opportunity here, however, for an interplay of use and extravagance, which takes shape in the solidity of the piece, without crevices for ease of cleaning, and the highly patterned surface and punctuating stone. Another area for relation of purpose to design has been that of the fish itself: the flowing lines of the tail and the regular patterns of gill and fin provide a natural contrast and tension within the piece, as does the juxtaposition of polished surface and chased detail."

Born: Dartford, Kent, 1967

Training and work: Kent Institute of Art and Design, BTech National Diploma, 1988; BTech Higher National Diploma, 1990; worked for silversmiths Ian Calvert, 1990–92, and Norman V. Bassant, 1992–93, to gain experience. Established a partnership with Steven Ottewill near Ashford, Kent, in 1993, where they do outwork for the London trade and designers, including Paul Belvoir, as well as their own line of jewellery and silverware designs and private commissions. Part-time teaching at Kent Institute of Art and Design.

First prize, Sandbourne Group UK Silver Awards; first prize, Business Design Centre Silversmithing design; two first prizes, for design and manufacture, Goldsmiths' Company Craft Competition; special award for outstanding design and craftsmanship, Goldsmiths' Company. Commissions for Lucy Cavendish College, Cambridge; Mercantile Credit Diamond Stakes trophy; and numerous others.

Justin and I met at the very hospitable location provided by the Crafts Council at Islington, London. Over a modest lunch we exchanged notes and ideas about the project, stimulated by Justin's enthusiasm and fervour for his vocation. My attention was first attracted to his work by his wonderful sense of design in the form of a pair of extraordinarily graceful and highly functional water jugs that were shown at the Crafts Council exhibition Twentieth-Century Silver *in the autumn of 1993.*

Fish slice
Sterling silver, lapis lazuli
London 1993
Length 13 in. (35 cm)
Weight 10.6 oz (331 g)

Server

Sterling silver

London 1994

Length 14 in. (35.5 cm)

Weight 11.9 oz (370 g)

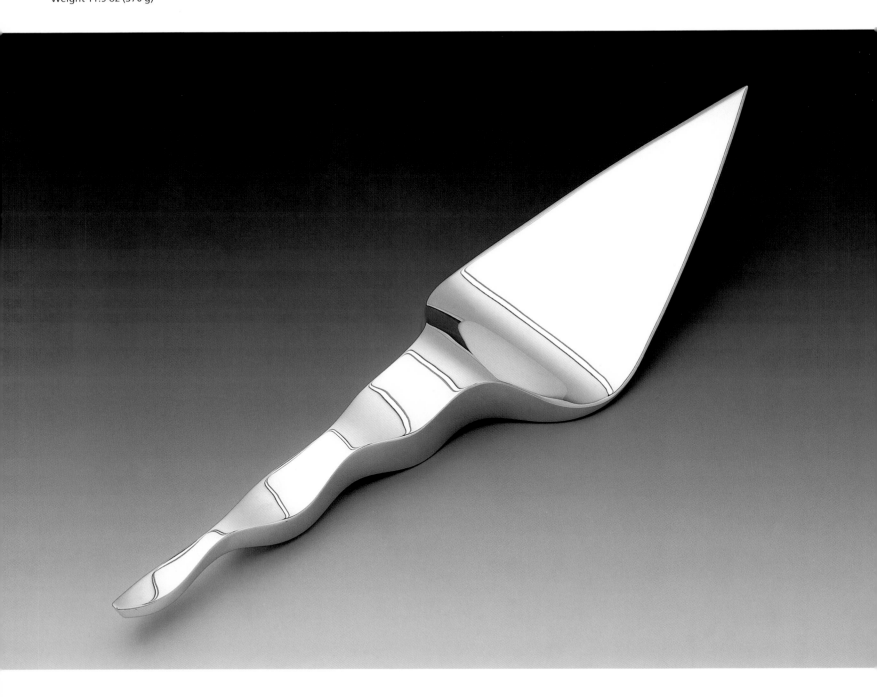

Toby Russell

The blade of this article is a severe trowel shape with straight sides. The rear edge enters a hollow construction with rounded shoulders and continuing apron into a hollow box handle. The handle is waved on all surfaces and tapers towards the end. It is in the vogue of Russell's invention of undulating silver surfaces generated by underside scoring and folding of the sheet metal while retaining a frame of definite edges and planes. The polished surfaces have a mirror finish.

Russell's technique is entirely innovative. It is not to be confused with flowing chased or electroformed styles. This piece may be compared to that of the American silversmith John Marshall (q.v.); both capture the ripple of water in form and line, both look for simplicity and clarity. In this server the regular curves of the handle contrast with the severe geometrical point of the blade; it is as if flowing water has been trapped in a cool, quiet, still pool. The transformation of curved to straight line is achieved through the union of handle and blade, as grip gives way to flat surface for reasons of function. This server presents a highly successful harmony of function and form.

Artist's philosophy/statement: "In my design for the silver cake slice I wanted to retain a simplicity of form, letting the line of the blade edge carry along the piece. The shape of the handle undulates, distorting reflections and enhancing the elegance of the shape while providing a tactile grip for the hand. Rather than relying on the surface detail I feel that the form alone should provide both function and aesthetic. The folds and curves of my designs on highly polished surfaces distort and transform reflections, enabling the piece to change according to the environment in which it is placed."

Born: London, 1963

Training and work: Camberwell School of Art, BA (Hons.) silversmithing and metalwork, 1982–86. Maker for Conran, New York.

Crafts Council grant, 1989; first prize, Craftsmanship and Design Award, Goldsmiths' Company and Crafts Council, 1993; Goldsmiths' Company Award, 1993; Humanity Prize Medal Competition, Royal Society of British Sculptors, 1993. Approximately fifty exhibitions and displays, mainly in England. Many commissions for colleges, the Goldsmiths' Company, churches and private collections.

I first saw Toby's work in the Crafts Council shop in Islington, London, where several of his highly original large pewter pieces were on display. The next near-contact was at a lunch in Goldsmiths' Hall, where a very large and striking vase, along with commissioned work of other smiths, decorated the table. We eventually met over coffee in Islington and shook hands over this project.

Jane Short

The server is in the form of a trowel. The heart-shaped blade is heavily engraved top and underside with swirling waves and currents. A central triangular area enamelled in blue-green depicts a mermaid rising from the deep and blowing seven fish up the enamelled and engraved handle. The blade is grasped by a split boss, triangular on top and a rounded 'V' underneath, and fastened by three 18k gold screws. The underside of the blade is counter-enamelled in a blue-green sea. The enamelling is *basse taille* over the engraving. The mermaid's head is outlined by a man-in-the-moon over a gold sun; snails and shells accentuate the marine motif.

The piece follows the eighteenth-century trowel form in shape but the decoration leaps forward in time. Short is part of an Arts and Crafts group within British silversmithing. Her server fits the comments of the greatest of the Arts and Crafts enamellers, Alexander Fisher. He describes how "All the bewildering surfaces, all the depths and lovelinesses that lie darkly in the waters of sea-caves, all the glistening lustre of gleaming gold or silver back and fin of fish, the velvet purple of sea anemone" are "waiting for expression in enamel".[27] Short's self-confessed aim is to "produce work which has such a richness or subtlety of colour that you can't help but look and keep wanting to look at it again and again".[28] This piece is the artist's first in which she has so successfully tried contrasting areas of enamel with engraved metal.

Artist's philosophy/statement: "I was glad of the opportunity to indulge myself in the use of rich colour and imagery that so suits the medium of enamel. ... The mermaid ... has been a symbol of our dreams and inner life. In this piece she represents the bounty of the seas, offering up some of her delicious riches for our table. The back of the slice is also enamelled, in pale watery colours to blend with the silver. The areas left silver are also carved and engraved to add to the overall decorative effect."

Born: South Molton, Devon, 1954
Training and work: Central School of Art, BA, 1972–75; Royal College of Art, 1976–79. Established workshop in 1979. Part-time instructor, Central School of Art, 1979–92. Visiting lecturer at several colleges and polytechnics, including Royal College of Art, Middlesex Polytechnic and Jerusalem. Enamel outworker for several silversmiths.

Royal College of Art travelling scholarship to Japan, 1979; Crafts Council grant, 1980. Freeman of the Goldsmiths' Company. Founder-member, British Society of Enamellers. Many one-person shows and group exhibitions. Work in collections of Victoria and Albert Museum, Goldsmiths' Hall, National Museum of Scotland, among others, and many commissions, including Lichfield Cathedral Collection, Lambeth Palace Chapel, Warden's cup, Goldsmiths' Company, P&O Makower Trust and other private collections.

My interest in Jane's work was excited by a most beautiful enamelled vase that I saw on display at the Goldsmiths' Hall in London. Jane and I met at our flat in London. Although she lives in Brighton, she was then teaching at the Central School of Art in London. Her enormous talent is masked by her quiet manner. Work on the server was interrupted by the happy event of the birth of her first-born.

Fish slice

Sterling silver, gold and enamel

London 1992

Length 13 in. (33 cm)

Total weight 12.9 oz (400 g)

Dennis Smith (and Gareth Harris)

This is the only double-bladed server in the collection. The lower sheet blade has a reversed trowel shape. The upper blade is a forged oxidized net that operates on a trigger-pull under the handle. The boss is a cast mask of a giant fish head that swallows a part-fish handle whose tail shows a remnant of a torn net. The under-pull, on a counter-spring, is a small, moulded, arched fish. It lifts the net from the lower blade, which is pierced with wave-form arcs.

This article has no historic precedent with regard either to blade shape or mechanism of operation. It is strictly a modern one-off. The technical aspect recalls the ingenious contraptions invented by Victorian entrepreneurs whose endeavours are recorded in the Patent Office. Here, too, is great humour. The problem of uniting blade with handle is solved with bravura, as fish-tail handle is swallowed by the mouth of the blade. Is there not here an echo of Gaudier Brzeska's marble sculpture of a bird swallowing a fish? The server has a powerful totemic presence, reminiscent of curious objects found in ethnographic collections whose strangeness draws us to them like a magnet.

Artist's philosophy/statement: Smith "believes that the merit of an object, whether functional or decorative, stands on its visual appeal if decorative, or enjoyment of use if functional". In this case the employment has both visual and functional appeal.

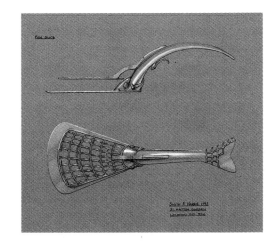

Born: London, 1953

Training and work: Sir John Cass School of Art, diploma in silversmithing, 1972; worked at Sir John Cass and then for Padgett & Braham Ltd. Formed Smith & Harris (with Gareth Harris) in 1981 in Hatton Garden, in a workshop that has been used by silversmiths since 1830. Hatton Garden is itself the centre of the London jewellery and diamond trade.

Many distinguished commissions, including The Silver Trust 10 Downing Street Collection for cigar boxes; an Oppenheimer-sponsored trophy for the King George VI and Queen Elizabeth Diamond Stakes at Ascot, made in a revolutionary triangular shape that opens three ways; vinaigrettes for a Middle Eastern client; and numerous others.

I first met Dennis and his colleague Gareth Harris in their underground workshop in Hatton Garden, London. Its crowded interior is a survival of the old 1830s workshop. While both are excellent craftsmen they have different talents: Gareth was trained as a box-maker and is the business manager, while Dennis is the mechanical wizard and designer, and in this case devised the special construction of the spring-and-trigger-pull as well as the whole design. They evidently work very well together.

Fish slice

Sterling silver

London 1994

Length 15 in. (38 cm)

Weight 14.9 oz (464 g)

Graham Stewart

The server takes the form of an abstracted flying fish. The blade is a complete ellipse. It is totally decorated with scales, and waves, and flying-fish-fin engraving, brought out dramatically by apt piercing. The handle is mounted as a rising fish tail, with wing-like effect, and is engraved with scales and close lines over its surface.

Although the elliptical blade harks back to the long oval server of the latter part of the eighteenth century, this piece is obviously quite modern in inspiration and connects directly to Stewart's devotion to nature. It recalls his attraction to these elegant animals and their graceful flight. The slice has a dramatic dynamism that has little to do with the static conceptions of centuries past. It exhibits a strong sense of pattern, combining fin and scale references with strikingly simple form. The alignment of lateral fin pattern with the tail of the handle creates a 'speed whisker' effect; the form seems to be flying – and conjures up the image of the flying fish. Action and movement are waiting to be released, giving the server an exciting tension.

Artist's philosophy/statement: "We set out to make works of lasting beauty, worthy of the finest materials; to respect and celebrate creation by responding through our eyes and hands. 'Does the man make the work or the work make the man?'" This particular expression was inspired by Stewart's lasting impression of these creatures as seen in their own habitat.

Born: Bridge of Allan, Scotland, 1955

Training and work: Gray's School of Art, Aberdeen, DA, 1973–77; post-DA, 1977–78. Apprentice work with Norman Grant, Fife, Malcolm Appleby (q.v.), and Roger Doyle, London. Established workshop in Dunblane, Scotland, 1978.

Postgraduate scholarship, Gray's School of Art, 1977; Gertrud Hector travelling scholarship, 1978. Freeman of the Goldsmiths' Company, 1996. Group and one-man exhibitions at museums and galleries in Scotland, England and USA. His work is in the collections of the Royal Scottish Museum and Goldsmiths' Hall. Commissions for royalty, clergy, Stirling University, Paisley University, the Thistle cup for Japan (the largest piece of silver hallmarked in Scotland), Parliamentarian of the Year, Mel Gibson, the BBC and others.

Graham and I first met at a Goldsmiths' Fair at the Hall. His excellent smithing and beautiful engraving immediately beckoned. Moreover, I was drawn by his forthright, modest manner. He is a lover and discoverer of nature. He finds inspiration for his work everywhere – as in a beaker that he made, inspired by the barley stooks that he recalled seeing in the fields at harvest time on one of the Scottish isles. He works in a family tradition: his father was an industrial designer and silversmith.

Fish slice

Sterling silver

Edinburgh 1992

Length 12 in. (30.5 cm)

Weight 17.4 oz (553 g)

Fish slice

Sterling silver

London 1996

Length 12 ¼ in. (31 cm)

Weight 9.2 oz (286 g)

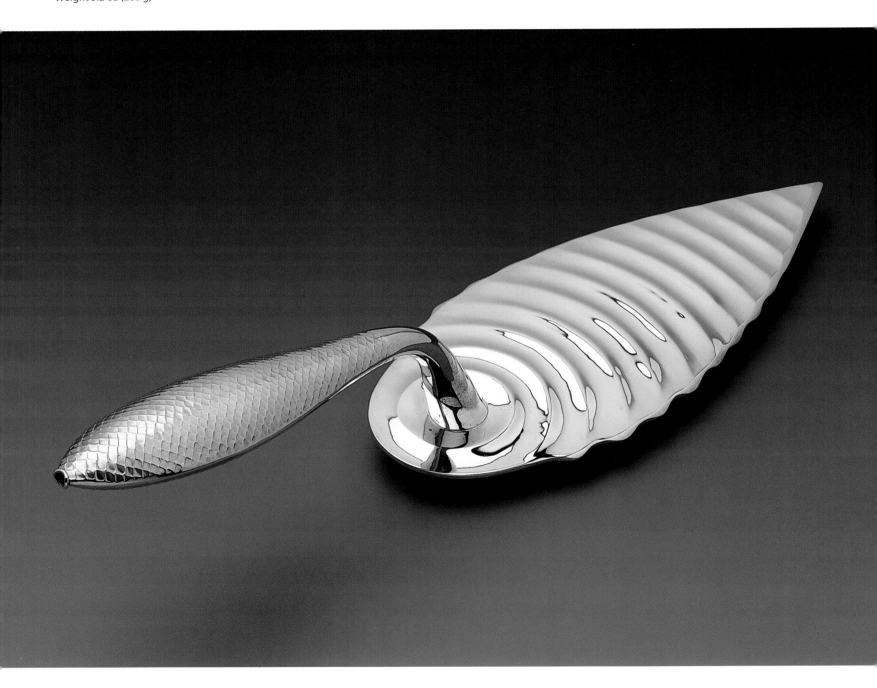

Lucian Taylor

The blade is a fourteen-gauge (1.6 mm) round-shouldered trowel. It has chased waves over the whole surface, scalloped edges and a rounded rear edge. The hollow, tapering, tubular stem lifts from the rear of the blade as an abstracted, oblate, oval, fish handle; the latter, ornamented with an all-over chased diaper scale pattern, tapers at both ends and represents an idealized fish leaping from the water. A finial is absent, leaving a novel mouth-like terminal orifice.

From the rippling waters of the blade a fish jumps out, leaping into the hand to form the handle. This dynamic quality is realized by the suggestion of water and rippling, and of fish by scale patterning. This server has a powerful simplicity created through a subtle suggestiveness and delicate balance of forms. The irregular navette of the pool of water is balanced by the fish handle. The 'fish' jumps out of the water with such speed that fin and tail are invisible; the flash of action has been captured as if in a camera shot.

Artist's philosophy/statement: "My work is only truly complete when it is employed. To this end I … aim to seduce hand and eye with form and texture. My designs are influenced by the purpose of an object … I enjoy working within the context of that which has gone before, playing both with and against tradition … The satisfaction of being both designer and a maker is due to the creative process not being limited to paper, but extending into the execution … I have as much to learn from my material as I have to teach it."

Born: London, 1967

Training and work: Bolton Institute of Higher Education, certificate in art and design, 1985–86; Brighton Polytechnic, 3-D design, BA (Hons.) first class, 1989; Royal College of Art, metalwork and jewellery, MA, 1992; University of Brighton, postgraduate design technology, 1993–94.

BP International Award for design, 1990; first prize, Royal Mint Medal Competition, 1991; second prize, Goldsmiths' Company Table Silver Competition, 1994; Crafts Council grant, 1995; second prize, Goldsmiths' Company Senior Silversmiths, 1996. Many exhibitions at galleries and museums in London, Paris and Munich. Commissions for the Shakespeare Globe Trust, Goldsmiths' Company, British Art Medal Society and the Royal Mint. Taylor's work has been the subject of many citations in magazines, newspapers and on television.

Lucian's work first came to my attention when I saw his prize-winning salt on display at Goldsmiths' Hall, London, in 1995. I was happy to offer him a commission at our first meeting at the Chelsea Crafts Fair in that year. This lovely article fulfilled my expectations that a carefully crafted, well-designed and original implement would result.

Alfred Ward

Called a fish server by its maker, this is obviously a very versatile article. This imposing implement has a modified trowel shape; an asymmetric rear edge displays a kick on the left side and a rearward projection on the right. This projection holds a rising (lifting) triangular boss that carries on as the wooden handle-holder. The blade has a long, forward-pointed, inscribed, oval reserve, within which there is an engraved pattern of diamonds, each one of which is centred by an oval pierced shape. There are seven tiers of such holes and a pierced tip triangle. The handle is triangular in cross-section and has a centred silver spine plate to which are pinned the handle pieces. The handle terminates in a triangular butt plate.

Ward's love of the metal, its versatility and malleabilty, his manipulation of the material, and his support of handcrafts and opposition to industry, put him within the Arts and Crafts tradition. His mastery of a large range of metalworking and decorative techniques means that his pieces often incorporate many different skills to a very high standard. The gentle curve of the handle echoes that of the 'cutting edge' of the blade and creates a satisfying unity of great integrity and grace.

Artist's philosophy/statement: "Many traditional skills of the silversmith are being lost and replaced by the mass-production methods of modern industry. My work reflects the use of classical silversmithing materials and techniques in the production of contemporary pieces. The forms exemplify my continued fascination with metal as a 'plastic' medium. Although I utilize hard-edge qualities within each piece, they are always complemented by fluid textural contrasts. Hollowing and raising, box-making and hand-engraving are rarely seen in today's metalsmithing arena. In addition to my personal direction in silversmithing, it is my desire to broaden an awareness of the craft among young designers and the general public."

Born: Dartford, Kent, 1942

Training and work: Canterbury College of Art, diploma in design and first class Hons. in silversmithing and jewellery, 1962; Birmingham University, Art Teacher's Diploma, 1963; City and Guilds of London Institute, certificate in silversmithing and engraving, 1965. He has taught at a number of schools and colleges, including the Kingsheath Technical School, 1963–65; Shoreditch College of Education, 1965–74; Chairman, Department of Silversmithing and Jewellery, City of London Polytechnic, 1974–81; University of Michigan Summer Program, 1983–85; Director, Ervin Crafts Center, Tennessee Technological University, 1985–89; Professor and Chairman, Art and Design, Winthrop University, South Carolina, 1989– . Designer for Barker Ellis Silver Company, 1963–73; for Spink & Son Ltd, 1973–81; and for The British Craftsman, 1981–85.

National finalist, Platinum Jewellery Design Competition, 1984. Major commissions for churches, universities, civic authorities and trophies in UK and USA.

Although I have not yet had the opportunity to meet Professor Ward, we have had a close encounter. It turns out that our paths almost crossed many years before. I took my first course in silversmithing in 1978 at the Sir John Cass School of Art when on sabbatical leave at University College London. My beneficent instructor was John Norgate, a talented box-maker. By coincidence, Ward was head of the Metalwork Department at that time. We did not meet, nor did I ever dream that he would one day make a piece for me. A telephone call and letter to South Carolina, together with repeated assurance of independence of design, resulted in this bold implement.

Server
Sterling silver, ebony handle
Rock Hill, South Carolina, 1994
Length 14 ¾ in. (37.5 cm)
Total weight 11.6 oz (360 g)

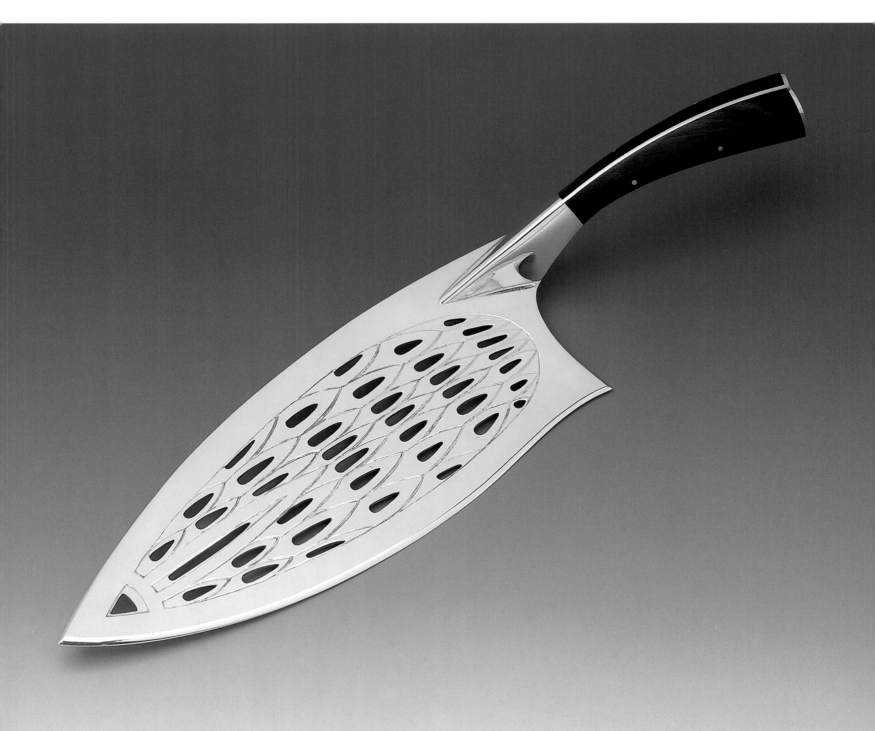

Fish slice
Sterling silver, gold wire
Edinburgh 1998
Length 9 ½ in. (24 cm)
Weight 18.7 oz (582 g)

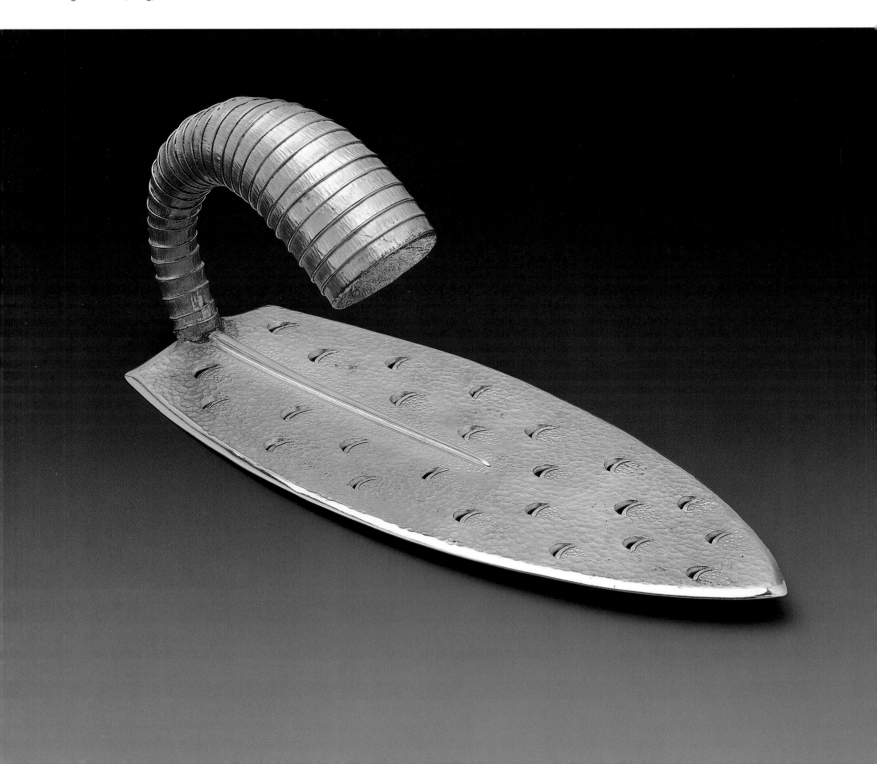

Julie Whitelaw

The server blade, of long oval shape with straight rear edge, is a hammered sheet with a projecting tang that enters a hollow handle, where it is soldered and pinned. The blade is pierced over the whole surface with lunettes, each emphasized by an impressed gold wire; it is strengthened by a long (5 in.; 12.5 cm), upper-surface rat-tail. The blade underside is uniformly chased with small rounds. All edges of the blade are bevelled. The handle is a forward-arching horn made of halves formed from 0.7 mm sheet and soldered together. The surface of this structure is covered with twenty-eight segments of narrow, overlapping, hammered bands, each edged with gold wire. The horn is closed with a cap covered with textured gold leaf.

This is an 'ancient and fish-like' server that reminds us of fossil forms. This piece revels in the possibilities of texture. The hollow handle is ribbed and gilded. The rich detail of the handle is counterpoised by the simple navette shape of the solid blade, which is patterned with rippling pools. Blade and handle are joined visually via a raised rib, like a rat-tail. This server captures the spirit of a primeval form.

Artist's philosophy/statement: "Silversmithing allows me to exploit the properties of the metal, such as its malleability, and to create interesting and tactile forms. Whenever possible I like to use structure as part of the design and to emphasize the three-dimensional form with textures and hammered surfaces."

Born: Lytham, Lancashire, 1955

Training and work: Duncan of Jordanstone College of Art, Dundee, art and design, graduated 1978; graduate apprenticeship scheme, Goldsmiths' Company, 1979; associate lecturer, Cleveland College of Art and Design, 1980– ; teaching diploma, New College, Durham, 1982; established workshop, Cleveland Crafts Centre, 1984– .

Many exhibitions in London, England and Scotland, including Leeds City Art Gallery, Barbican Centre, *Dazzle*, Newcastle Arts Centre and Edinburgh International Festival; Millennium Canteen project, Sheffield; founder-member, Association of British Designer Silversmiths.

After seeing the fish server that Julie had made for the Millennium Canteen, and after several telephone conversations and exchanges of information, I asked her to make a slice for me. We met in London six months later when she delivered the server.

Pastry slice
Sterling silver
Edinboro, Pennsylvania, 1996
Length 10 in. (25.5 cm)
Weight 9.5 oz (296.5 g)

The server blade is made as a flower and the handle as a jointed stem of a member of the heliconia plant family, *Nickeriensis*. The lightly textured handle is cast; the polished flower was assembled by soldering together the various petals, each of which is thereby unique in shape. This article does not have cutting capability and is obviously a stabber or lifter for the service of small cakes, pastries *etc*. The folded-back stem supplies a very comfortable and remarkably beautiful and realistic handle.

This totally naturalistic creation is one of a number that grew out of the personal experience of the artist. In the spring of 1993 Sue travelled down the Amazon River in a dug-out canoe. The plant forms she saw were very beautiful and their impact was enhanced by the way they grew together and intertwined. The visual experience inspired her *Jungle* series. The boldness of this server's outline brings to mind the striking images of Karl Blossfeldt (1865–1932), whose black-and-white photographs of plants were such an inspiration to art metal-founders and modellers. This server captures the delicate form of an exotic bloom, bringing surprise and delight to the table. In the Renaissance it was customary to strew the tablecloth at lavish banquets with flowers. Perhaps this highly unusual server has appropriated some of that historical precedent.

Artist's philosophy/statement: "I want to create works that have a sense of beauty, fantasy and femininity, that might exist in an idealized world. … Plantlife has been a major source of inspiration for me. … I hope to capture their gesture and grace. Healthy plants are strong living organisms, yet their forms can be delicate and intricate. I find this contrast between delicacy and strength a compelling element of nature and use this contrast in my work."

Born: Youngstown, Ohio, 1963

Training and work: Miami University, OH, BFA, 1985; Indiana University, Bloomington, MFA, 1988; assistant, 1988, instructor, New York YMCA, 1988–90; head of jewellery, Buck's Rock, New Milford, CT, 1989; instructor, School of Visual Arts, New York, 1989–90; visiting assistant professor, Miami University, OH, 1990–91; associate professor, Edinboro University, PA, 1991– . Member of SNAG, American Craft Council, among other professional organizations.

Pye Scholarships, Miami University, 1982–83; Alumni travelling scholarship, 1985; National Society of Arts and Letters, IN, Bachmura Award, 1986, and Dickerson Award, 1987; Juror's Awards, Arrowmont School of Arts and Crafts, TN, 1990, 1992; merit award, *Anticipation '93*, Chicago 1993; Pennsylvania Council of Arts Fellowship, 1994; Mid-Atlantic Regional Fellowship, 1995; and other recognition. Numerous solo, group and invited exhibitions throughout the USA, Europe and Japan. Her work is in private and public collections, including the White House and museums. She has given many lectures, served on juries and conducted workshops at universities and museums. Her work has been the subject of reviews and articles in magazines and books.[1]

Suzanne's work became known to me through the many photographs and descriptions of it that appeared in the craft magazines. I was attracted by her style and was very pleased when, in a telephone conversation followed by a letter, she agreed to undertake this commission. The USA is so large that personal contact with each craftsperson was often impossible. For this reason in particular, I preferred the telephone to e-mail or fax for rapid communication, the spoken word, with its individual tone and timbre, being much more personal.

Phillip Baldwin

The broad knife-blade shape has a hammered raised right edge and is made of palladium sheet that has been etched in wave form to reveal the underlying silver base. The blade is pierced with a bubble design. The *mokumé gané* flat handle carries the swirling pattern in yet another mode. It is made of some nineteen alternating layers of the two metals. The handle rises from the rear edge and has a reverse S-scroll end shape.

Baldwin's blacksmithing background is readily apparent in the simple but strong and forceful nature of the shaping of this piece. At the same time, one sees the subtle but rich and varied texture of the surfaces – so characteristic of his steel knife blades. Simple in form and outline, the decorative richness of this server lies in the complex Japanese metalworking technique of *mokumé gané*. The process involves the bonding of various metals and alloys, resulting in decorative wood-grain effects. Baldwin combines a modernist appreciation of simplicity with a traditional technique that has been in use for some three hundred years. Past and present are united in this unusual reassessment of a very functional form.

Artist's philosophy/statement: "This work was about solving (my) conceptual conflicts rather than technical or formal problems. One of the conflicts revolved around the recognition of two strong, basic, philosophic influences. The first is Calvinist austerity; the second is a love of decoration and ornament that comes from the direct experience with the material and the pleasure that sensual experiences can give. A problem was the relationship of the austere to work of a rich and aristocratic nature. I became aware that only in work of this nature could I be challenged to use my abilities to their greatest extent. I appreciate the chance to do a work of this kind and the opportunity to resolve a set of conflicts that had been influencing me for years."

Born: New York, 1953

Training and work: State University College, Potsdam, NY, BA, 1976; State University, Stonybrook, 1976; Southern Illinois University, MFA, 1979. Established own studio with emphasis on knives and implements and mixed-metal work, 1967. Had experience in sculpture businesses, 1973–79; Oregon School of Arts and Crafts, resident craftsman in metals, 1979–81; founded Shining Wave Metals firm for production of exotic laminated metals, 1983– ; employed by Metal Arts Group, 1984–86. Frequent lecturer at the University of Washington.

He has given innumerable workshops and lectures throughout the US and published a number of articles on knives, *mokumé gané* and craft techniques.

Regents' Scholarship, New York, 1971; Museum merit award for jewellery, Evansville, IN, 1978; best of show, Illinois-Ozarks Craft Guild Exhibition, 1978; first prize in metals, Brooks Memorial Art Gallery, Memphis, 1978; American Craft Museum Design Award, 1985; honourable mention, Tacoma Art Museum, 1986; best craftsmanship award, Juried Conference Exhibition, Alfred, NY, 1990; work in many museum and private collections. Innumerable one-man and group exhibitions nationally and internationally. Many published articles. Baldwin has been the subject of reviews and articles in a number of national magazines.[2]

Phil Baldwin is a near-neighbour and acquaintance in Seattle. His workshop is rather like a great smithy – the counterpoint being the lovely textile studio of his wife, Layne Goldsmith. Phil is a moving force and spirit in the North-West and national metals and craft scene. He is a leading producer of mixed-metal materials.

Server

Blade of sterling-palladium bimetal;

handle of sterling-palladium *mokumé gané*

Snohomish, Washington, 1993

Length 11 ¼ in. (28.5 cm)

Total weight 7.7 oz (238 g)

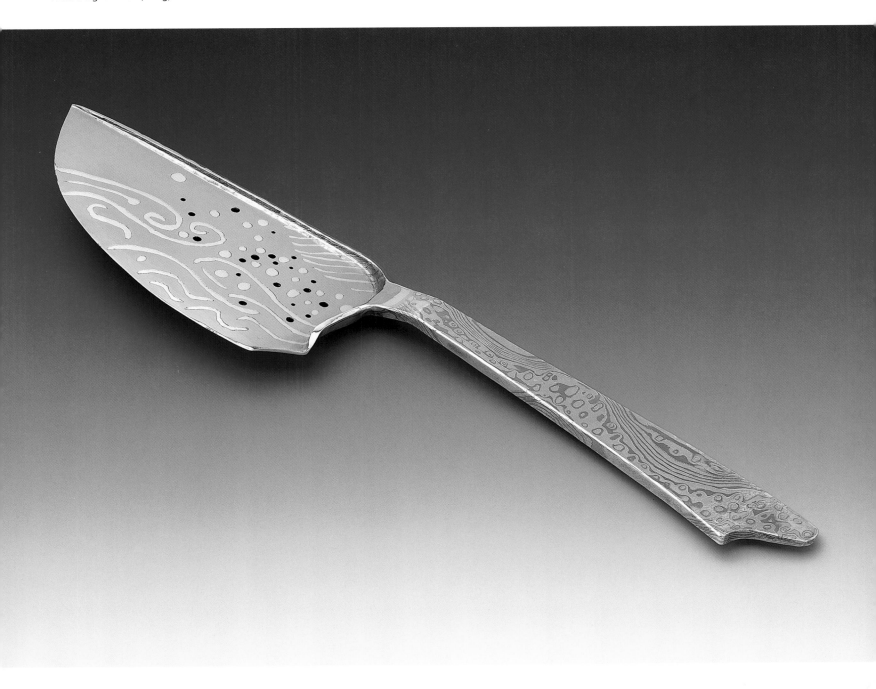

Fish slice

Sterling silver

Duvall, Washington, 1997

Length 11 in. (28 cm)

Weight 8.75 oz (272 g)

Candace Beardslee

blade top and bottom sides. The handle terminates in a spherical bulb from which long vine-like shoots fold down over the fronds.

The shape and decoration Beardslee chose for her server suggest a response to the brief similar to that of Cynthia Eid (q.v.). Both capture an aspect of life in the sea, one by association, the other by literal reference. Beardslee has used the idea of strands of seaweed for the handle, made separately from the blade. While Eid's blade curls up at the blade edge to scoop up the contents, Beardslee has pierced hers with five small ovals – like breathing-holes. The sinuous curves of the weed are reinforced by the whiplash line of a single wire of silver, which sprouts from the finial, reminiscent of Art Nouveau forms. The design is both stylized and naturalistic. It has great presence.

The blade is made in the shape of a *punctate pandora* clam shell. It carries five oval holes along the right edge, which is slightly rolled down; the left edge is chamfered. The blade is singly dished and cross-peened on its top surface, reminiscent of the uneven inner surface of the animal; the underside is completely chased with regular, parallel, elongated, semi-circular reeding that again follows life. The handle is inspired by the bull kelp, whose chased and ribbed fronds grasp the

Artist's philosophy/statement: "This server reflects some of the things that have influenced my art over the years, things that directly come from the North West environment. Puget Sound is one of the defining features of this area, a key ingredient in the beauty of the North West. The fish server seemed a perfect vehicle to reflect some of these values."

Born: Kirkland, Washington, 1949

Training and work: Cornish School of Arts, Seattle; Burnley School of Professional Arts, 1970; Central Washington University, art education, BA, 1974; University of Washington, MFA, 1995; art teacher, 1974–76; jewellery manager, Frederick & Nelson, Seattle, 1980–82; instructor, University of Washington, 1995; self-employed, 1982– ; member, SNAG.

Pacific Northwest Arts and Crafts Fair; Craft Exhibition Award, 1982; Active Arts Award, 1983; Craft Exhibition Award, 1984; Juror's Award, 1996. *Ornament* magazine International Competition, honourable mention, 1984; Whatcom Museum International Art Competition, Juror's Award, 1991; Design Arts Trust Fellowship, 1992; Felissimo Design Awards, NY, recognition prize, 1996; The Meadows Gallery, Denton, TX, Materials Hard and Soft Juror's Award, 1997. Numerous solo, group and invited exhibitions in galleries and museums in the USA and in Paris. Her work has been reviewed in *Metalsmith*, *Ornament* and *American Craft*.

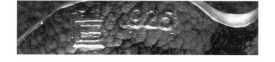

I know Candace personally and have seen her at work in the studio at the University of Washington while I laboured over some of my mistakes. Moreover, I had seen the beautiful result of her raising and chasing, most recently a prize-winning tea service. I was anxious to have her make a server for me.

Flora Book

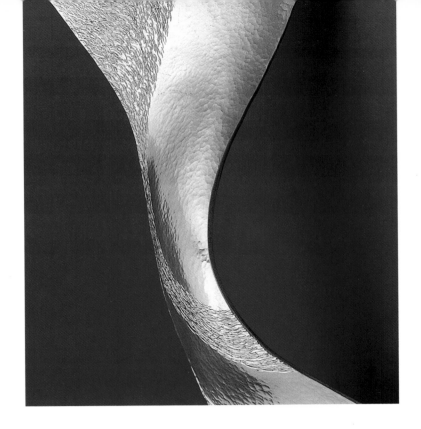

The server is forged from a single piece of fourteen-gauge (1.6 mm) sheet and is in the shape of an arching fish whose tail provides the handle. The animal is completely covered on both sides with a texture of swirled cross-peening and pouncing that delineates the anatomy of the fish while simultaneously enhancing the action motif of the overall shape and imbuing it with a water-wave environmental character. The left edge is bevelled. It is not pierced, but both its decoration and shape render such a doubtful practical requirement unnecessary.

This design, which ostensibly utilizes a standard and, in a sense, hackneyed fish shape, actually owes very little to history or precedence. It has a dynamic, fluid character that is uniquely the maker's characteristic method of working in her usual *métier*, jewellery. The server combines boldness of shape with intricate surface texturing, recalling the swirling and eddying of water; the fish is in its element. The raised tail fin transforms a flat pattern into a three-dimensional form. Like Andrea Schweitzer's server, this design solution is about capturing the essence of 'fishness'.

Artist's philosophy/statement: "I follow my own bent, but I can find new ideas wherever I look, whether it be ethnic work from another continent or some facet of everyday surroundings. My work practises technical simplicity."

Born: Perth Amboy, New Jersey, 1926

Training and work: Ohio University, BFA, 1948; further study at Concordia University, Montreal; San Miguel University, Mexico; University of Washington, Seattle, with Ramona Solberg, Mary Lee Hu and John Marshall (q.v.). Early training and artistic activity were in painting.

Tacoma Art Museum jewellery prize, 1986; Facere Gallery jewellery art prize, 1987; Denton Museum exhibition prize, 1992; Lafayette, LA, Art Association Prize, 1993; Bellingham Art Museum, North-West International Craft Prize, 1993; 47th North-West Annual Craft Prize, 1993; Beads on Target Prize, Alexandria, VA, 1995. Her jewellery work is included in the collections of several museums in the USA including: Metropolitan Museum, New York; Museum of Fine Arts, Boston; Renwick Gallery, Washington; and others. She has been featured in many one-person and group shows in galleries and museums in the USA and UK.[3]

The maker has been personally well known to the writer for over twenty years. He has always admired her original sense of design, which is her own unique creative force.

Fish slice

Sterling silver

Seattle, Washington, 1995

Length 13 in. (33 cm)

Weight 9.8 oz (304 g)

Cake slice

Sterling silver

Carlisle, Massachusetts, 1998

Length 12 ⅝ in. (32 cm)

Weight 18 oz (560 g)

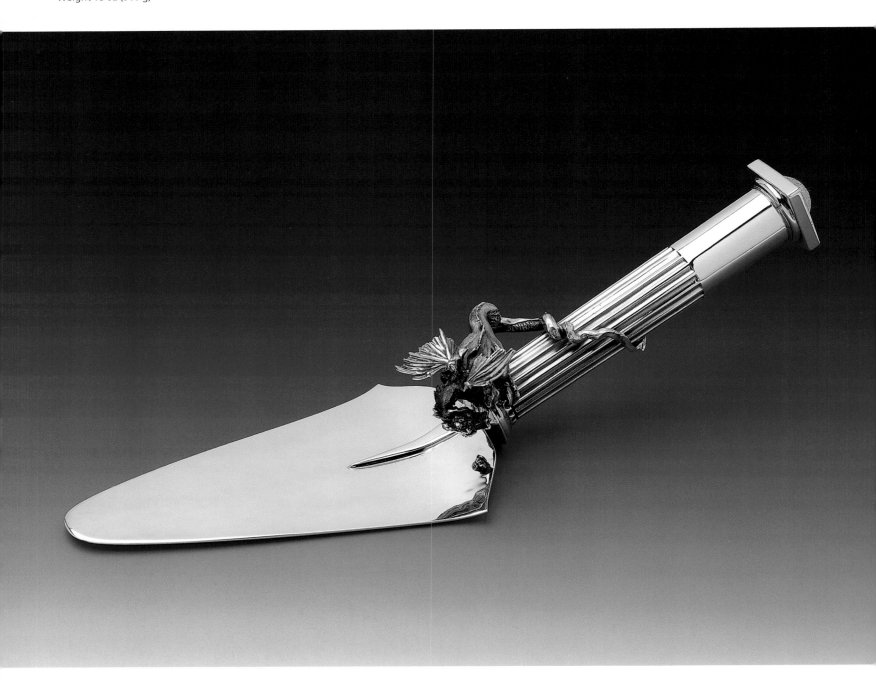

Michael Brophy

The server has a trowel shape and a lightly hammered blade with rounded tip and pointed rear side cusps. It bends up towards the back to a convex round, which holds a fluted, columnar handle. The blade is held by a small U-drop underneath and a short rat-tail topside, and is further secured by a bolt that passes into the hollow handle. The handle is fluted over two-thirds of its forward length and terminates in a heavy square capital, from which a finely peened, starburst, quarter-round finial button protrudes. The junction end of the handle is surmounted by a ferocious winged dragon whose tail writhes back over and along the column and whose claws scar the round that holds the blade.

Brophy's server belongs in a science-fiction fantasy. The detailed and elaborate cast creature writhes with disturbing life. Its knotted muscles and snaking tail contrast with the polished smoothness and glitter of the columnar handle. This might be a tool to be used in an alien banquet, disturbing and delighting in equal measure.

Artist's philosophy/statement: "I am a designer/developer … of functional objects. I primarily design pieces specifically for an event or individual, which means conceptualizing the object with input from the customer … It gives me the greatest satisfaction to know that the customer has been at least partially involved in the aesthetic result. As a craftsman my strength lies in my technical interest and ability, coupled with a personal need to make the quality of things extremely well … What I design and make has to be perfectly functional and visually easy to interpret."

Born: New York, 1959

Training and work: Medway College of Design, Chatham, Kent, UK, diploma, 1978–82, graduated with distinction. Worked in London at Grant MacDonald International, 1982–84; had own workshops in London, 1984–85. Returned to USA, to Colonial Williamsburg Foundation, VA, 1985–88; established own manufactory and design studio, 1988– . Work for Reed & Barton, Steuben Glass, Gorham, Lunt, Tiffany, among others.

Goldsmiths' Company Craftsman of the Year Award; Johnson-Matthey Metal Company Award. Many commissions for churches, museums and institutions, including: Church of St Peter's Cross Keys; St John's College, Cambridge; Christ Church, Chesapeake, VA; Harvard University; University of Colorado; Goldsmiths' Company; US State Department; De Beers; sporting trophies, including Ascot, Indianapolis 500, PGA trophies; and numerous architects, including Robert Venturi.

I have not yet had the pleasure of meeting Michael although we have mutual acquaintances in the British craft world. We have held many telephone conversations.

Robert Butler

The server is a beautifully modelled, cast and chased assemblage of marine motifs. The blade is a realistic flounder that is wonderfully pierced over the whole body – apart from ruffled fins and head – to form the scales in negative. The handle is a cast complex: a squid holds the tail of the flounder in its tentacles, and is itself being attacked by a voracious eel whose body is nibbled by a realistic fish with highly oxidized brown eyes. The central part of the flounder body is ten to twelve gauge (2.5 mm) and comes down to twenty gauge (0.8 mm) on fins and head, which act as serving edges.

This server is as much a piece of table sculpture as a practical dining implement. Butler's skills as a modeller and caster have created a deliciously complex piece that has all the surprise of a Palissy dish, a piece of contemporary baroque. The cast marine creatures also call up images of the modelling of the French eighteenth-century Rococo silversmiths, for example Thomas Germain (1673–1748) and Juste-Aurèle Meissonnier (1695–1750), whose tureens were topped by silver fishes, shells and crabs, some of them cast from life.

Artist's philosophy/statement: "It always has been important to me that the skill and art of silversmithing combine to create work that is as functional as it is graceful. In this commission I was able to combine four distinct silversmithing disciplines: modelling, forging, chasing and piercing. Combining these particular techniques, however, imposed technical challenges that I enjoyed solving. For instance, the best way to make a utensil like the fish slice is to forge it. Forging, however, usually limits design because forgings are hardened through hammering yet *softened* with heat. Applying cast decorative elements (such as the cast fish handle) to a forging (like the blade) runs the risk of weakening the overall integrity of the piece. I decided to approach this problem by making the forged blade heavier than usual. Then I chased and pierced the blade with a fish-scale pattern. This lightened it yet maintained its strength – keeping the fish slice functional and not merely decorative."

Born: Hanover, New Hampshire, 1955

Training and work: Apprenticeship in silversmithing with Michael Murray, London, 1972–76; courses in chasing and engraving, Sir John Cass School of Art, London, 1974–76. Employed by Sarah Jones, 1975–76; Gebelein Silversmiths, Boston, 1976–77; opened workshop, 1977, specializing in raising, modelling, piercing and chasing. He is a member of several professional and cultural societies.

A number of exhibitions at museums and galleries; technical advisor and guest lecturer, Museum of Fine Arts, Boston. Commission for Museum of Fine Arts, Boston, and many private commissions.

After speaking to Robert many times by telephone, we finally met at the exhibition of the collection at Goldsmiths' Hall, London, in September 1995. It was a pleasure to meet the person behind the name, or in this case, the voice. Robert very helpfully shared with me his knowledge of the London silversmithing scene.

Fish slice

Sterling silver

Pine Plains, New York, 1994

Length 15 in. (38 cm)

Weight 16.9 oz (526 g)

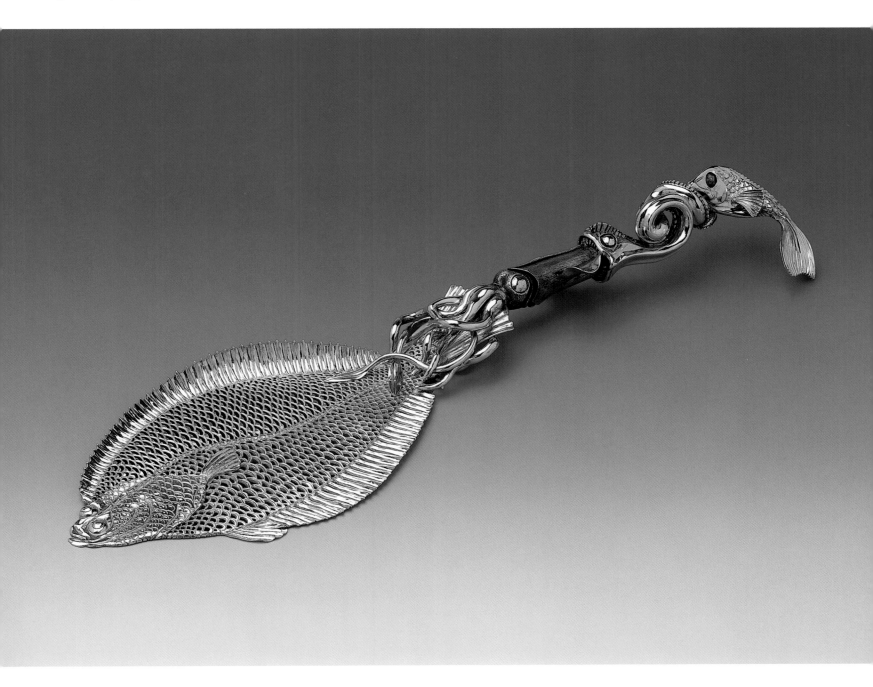

Fish slice
Sterling silver and lapis lazuli
Houston, Texas, 1993
Length 13 ¾ (35 cm)
Total weight 8.6 oz (267 g)

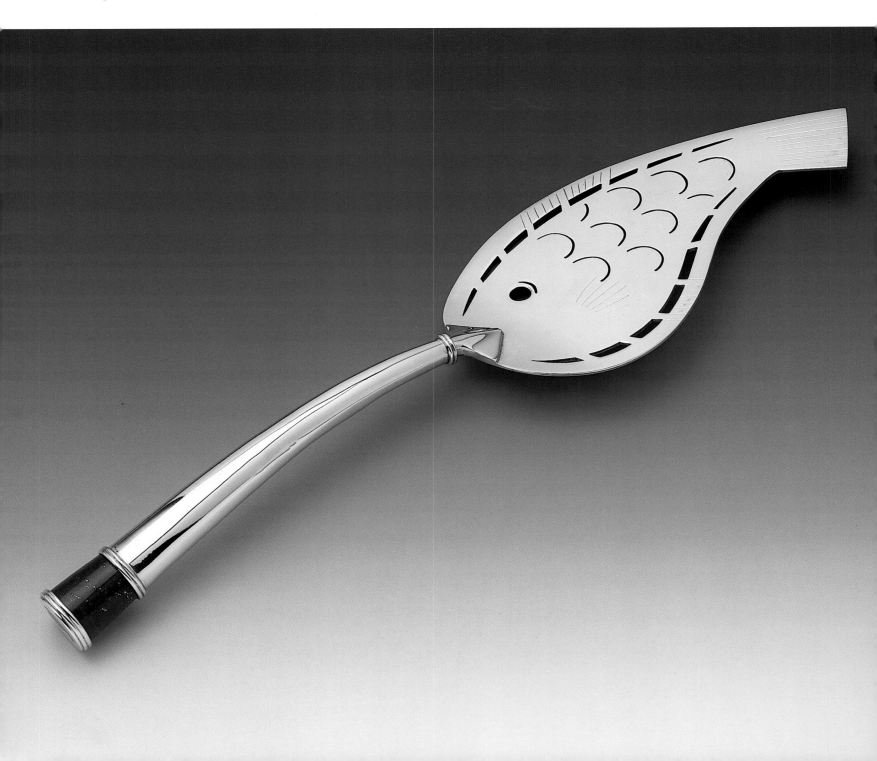

Wade Callender

The server takes the novel shape of an idealized flat-sheet fish on a line. The fish is of simple outline with minimal piercing and engraving to evoke the animal. The anticlastic fishing-rod handle is attached to the blade by a triangular boss. It terminates in a cylindrical lapis lazuli finial that carries a sterling end-cap with a companion fish-shaped cut-out.

This implement follows a minimalist style while working out a pleasing design. Quite uniquely, the point of the blade is provided by the fish tail rather than the head. The lapis stone evokes the sea colour. This simple server has all the strength and vitality of Art Deco, with its taste for solid rectilinear shapes, bold strong patterns and quasi-geometrical dissection of forms. Art Deco was a luxury style; this server exploits the brilliant sheen that silver can take, with the richness of lapis lazuli.

Artist's philosophy/statement: "Being a minimalist at heart, my designs generally have clean lines with a very limited number of elements in the composition. Almost all work is done by fabrication, using techniques such as shell forming (particularly anticlastic sinking as exemplified by the work of Heikki Seppa and Michael Good), forging, raising, the hydraulic press *etc*. Chasing and *repoussé* are also used but primarily in a geometric rather than organic fashion. The metal-forming techniques used emphasize the fluidity and movement that can be achieved with metals and require particular attention in incorporating stones into the design. In many cases the lapidary work must be completed after fitting the stone into the metal design. Using the minimalist approach requires careful attention to the finishing and polishing of both the metal and stone components."

Born: North Kingsville, Ohio, 1926

Training and work: College of Wooster, BA, 1948 University of Rochester, PhD, physical chemistry, 1951. Dr Callender is a physical chemist who turned metalsmith as a continuing career after his retirement from the Shell Chemical Co. in 1988. He first became interested in jewellery work in 1970. His training has been informal, first with Pat McCrary (PM Limited), 1983, then extensively with Val Link at the University of Houston, 1986–94. Coursework at the Glassell School of Art, 1989–90. He instructs part-time at the University of Houston. He formed his own company, WADE, in 1988.

First prize, flatware, National Student Silverware Competition, 1990. First prize, jewellery design, Houston Gem Society, 1991–92, 1995. Exhibitions at Christie's, NY; Tiffany, NY; Coeur d'Alene and Boise, ID; and other galleries and venues. Various commissions.

I contacted Wade when he came to my notice as the flatware prize winner in the National Student Silverware Competition of 1990, a great distinction. I was amazed to learn that he was a physical chemist who had done his PhD thesis research in my own field of chemical kinetics with scientists of my acquaintance, and was almost of my own vintage. As a late hobbyist and student, he became a superior craftsman and designer of great ability and competence. I finally had the pleasure of meeting Wade and his wife at an exhibition of the collection at the National Ornamental Metals Museum, Memphis, Tennessee, in 1996.

Chunghi Choo

The server is an abstracted fish shape made from sheet silver. The blade is an extended oval plate with a bifurcated sharp-pointed mouth that carries out the theme of the shape. It is pierced in a fly-away pattern. The blade lifts to a two-tier handle, each side of which is in four plane pieces that convey a strong dynamic effect. The two tiers are separated and stabilized by eight post-pins.

The server is a classic study in minimalism and creative design. It is a piece of sculpture rather than a functional article. It is a masterpiece of design conception that creates beauty for the eye. The squid-like form has a very powerful visual identity. While the handle invites the grasping hand, the strength and almost aggressiveness of the form hold the viewer back. There is a tremendous tension and excitement in this piece. Its power derives from a simplification of form, and an intense interest in detail. The wave- or fin-like fretted pattern in the blade pushes up and down, creating a sea-like ebb and flow.

Artist's philosophy/statement: Choo captures her joyful creations in sensuous forms and beguiling surfaces … simplicity, harmony and tranquillity are integral to her work. … Choo speaks of harmony in life and art: "Music helps me to make my work harmonious, joyous and flowing – like the music itself. … I like to see in my work simplicity and grace and I like for each piece to appear sensuous and celebratory."[4]

Born: Inchon, Korea, 1938

Training and work: Ewha Women's University, Seoul, BFA, Oriental painting 1961; Cranbrook Academy of Art, Michigan, MFA, 1965. Other study at Penland School of Crafts, NC, and Tyler School of Art, PA. Instructor, University of Northern Iowa, Cedar Falls, 1965–68; University of Iowa, Iowa City, 1965– ; presently professor and head of jewellery and metalsmithing; visitor, Crafts Department, New School of Social Research, New York, 1975–76, and Arrowmont School of Arts and Crafts, Gatlinburg, TN, 1978.

Many prizes, best-of-show citations and honourable mentions in juried exhibitions for her work in textiles and in metals. Frequent reviews and citations of innumerable invitational exhibitions, both one-person and group, in newspapers, magazines and books. Her work is in the collections of museums in the USA and elsewhere, including: Metropolitan Museum of Art, New York; Victoria and Albert Museum, London; Musée des Arts Decoratifs, Paris; Art Institute of Chicago; and many other collections, public and private. She has been cited as well for her teaching excellence and has served as juror for many competitions and exhibitions. She has published and also been the subject of many articles, and has presented many lectures and workshops, in the USA and abroad.

I finally had the pleasure of meeting Professor Choo at a SNAG conference in Seattle in 1998. I was attracted to her work by a stunning bowl that came with a touring exhibition of silverwork to the Bellevue Art Museum, Washington. Thereafter we communicated by letter and by telephone. Her 'drawing' was a silvered cardboard model of her intention – impressive!

Fish slice
Sterling silver
Iowa City, Iowa, 1993
Length 17 in. (43 cm)
Weight 12.7 oz (396 g)

Fish slice

Sterling silver

Clintondale, New York, 1997

Length 10¾ in. (27.5 cm)

Weight 13.5 oz (421 g)

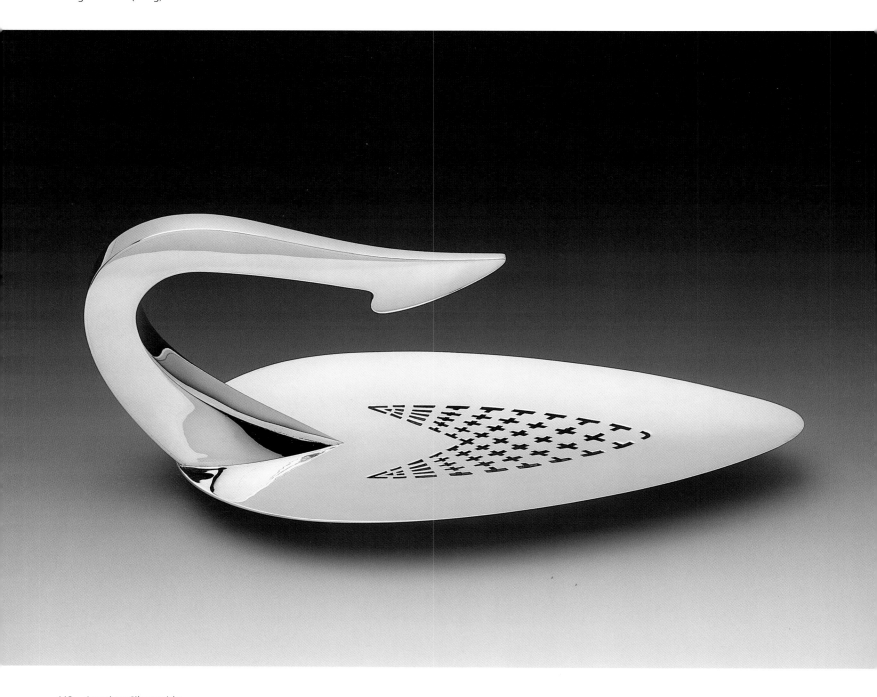

John Cogswell

The server is derived from a fish lure, as is made evident by the barbed handle. It is one of several in the collection (see Musgrove and Whitelaw) in which the handle turns back towards the blade, and again proves to have excellent balance. The blade is a highly rounded trowel shape, dished around the long axis and pierced with a diaper pattern of crosslets in an arrow-head shape. The hollow four-sided handle rises as a long V-shape on the blade and sweeps up and turns forward. All surfaces are polished.

The design of this server derives from the maker's avid interest in fishing, and is quite appropriate for a fish server. The barb of the handle complements the forward thrust of the tip of the blade, creating an impression of live and sinuous tension. This elemental power is undisturbed by ornament. Even the piercing is simple and functional, the crosses and lines reinforcing the dynamic V-shape at fore and aft. This is silver at its most simple and sculptural. Its power lies in the harmony of scale, shape and form.

Artist's philosophy/statement: "In an age of machine technology, I choose to spend my life making things by hand. I choose *not* to resign myself to a world of mass-produced, stamped-out 'tinware'. I create, therefore I am. In the manner that the cultural legacy of fine art and crafts has been passed down through the generations, my work is hand-formed and fabricated using … traditional tools and techniques … . As a metalsmith, I am one link in a living chain, a metalsmithing tradition stretching from antiquity into the future. I am a teacher and an object-maker. I take very seriously the responsibility of nurturing and passing on the skills and knowledge entrusted to me. The objects which issue forth from my heart and my hands are, to me, an affirmation of my humanity."

Born: Cortland, New York, 1948

Training and work: State University of New York (SUNY), Cortland, 1966–68; SUNY, New Paltz, gold- and silversmithing, BFA, 1979; MFA, 1984; SUNY, teaching assistant, 1981, lecturer, 1984–85; Pratt Institute, New York, visiting associate professor, 1987–88; Parsons School of Design, New York, instructor, 1992– ; Hofstra University, adjunct assistant professor, 1993–94. Designer-silversmith, Fiorentini Jewelers Inc., Cortland, NY 1968–76; designer, K.J.M. Silversmiths Inc., New Paltz, 1979– ; studio jeweller/ silversmith, 1979– ; director, jewellery and silversmithing department, YM/YWHA, New York City, 1985– . Over one hundred workshops and seminars at venues around the USA and Canada. Member, Arrowmont board of governors advisory committee; past member, Brookfield Craft Creator board of trustees. Member, Society of American Silversmiths, SNAG, American Craft Council, Empire State Crafts Alliance, Florida Society of Goldsmiths.

Bennett Memorial Art scholarship, 1978; Haystack scholarship, 1979. Approaching one hundred exhibitions, one-man and group shows at museums, galleries, universities and colleges around the USA. Many private commissions; public commissions include State University of New York, New Paltz; Cortland, NY, County Arts Council; Jewish Museum, New York City; Kohler Arts Center, Sheboygan, WI.

I came to know of John's talents through his friend and former mentor Kurt Matzdorf (q.v.). We spoke by telephone and came rapidly to agreement.

Cynthia Eid

The server is formed in one piece by deft twisting of the fourteen-gauge metal. The surface is cross-peened topside, and brushed and polished on the underside. The term 'pudding' slice is of eighteenth-century origin. This server exemplifies what a pudding-cum-casserole-cum-vegetable server should be. The narrow folded-back right side of the blade provides enough of a spoon effect (an association also ascribed to some eighteenth-century trowels; see chapter 3) to make this function so practical.

This slice is an example of minimalist design that could lend itself to commercial production. It is devised and executed from a single piece of silver, enforcing a strong and coherent unity in design. The handle seems to be extruded from the blade, twisting like a tail, or a rope of seaweed. The effective simplicity of the form is engagingly complicated by the surface treatment. The elaborately peened/chased surface evokes an indefinable range of organic resonances: the texture creates ripples of light, like sunshine on water. Strength of form and delicacy of decoration are in perfect balance. Compare with the server by Beardslee (q.v.).

Artist's philosophy/statement: "Most of my work is hammer-formed. I love the evolutionary transformation from the flat sheet toward an object of unity, fluidity and serenity. I enjoy stretching the limits of convention for utilitarian objects, but it is important that each functions well. People often react to an object I've made by associating it with a natural form they can put a name to. ... The form of this server has its roots in my garden, as well as my meanderings in, on and along the edges of water and woods. The destiny I would like for each of my pieces is to inhabit someone's living or working space, to be held and contemplated for a moment's respite from the hectic world."

Born: Madison, Wisconsin, 1954

Training and work: University of Wisconsin, Madison, BS art education, 1977; Indiana University, Bloomington, MFA jewellery, design and metalsmithing, 1980. Associate instructor, Indiana University, 1978–80; instructor, Lexington Arts and Crafts Society, MA, 1992–94; metalsmithing instructor, De Cordova Museum, Lincoln, MA, 1995– . Design/goldsmith, Joel Bagnal Goldsmith, Wellesley, MA, 1980–81, and Neal Rosenblum, Worcester, MA, 1981; modelmaker, designer, supervisor, Verilyte Inc., Brookline, MA, 1982–85; freelance metalsmith, 1985– .

Best in show, Madison, WI, 1975; Ford Foundation grant, 1977; Judge's Award, Containers, Bloomington, IN, 1978; third prize, Silver Design Competition, New York, 1978; Metal Award, Beaux Arts Designer Craftsman, Columbus, OH, 1979; Flatware Award, Silver Design Competition, New York, 1980; finalist, Spertus Judaica Prize, 1996; Silverhawk National Fine Crafts Competition, secondary award, metal, 1996, primary award, jewellery/metal, 1996, metal award, 1997; Juror's Award, Crafts National 31, Pennsylvania State University, 1997. Approaching one hundred shows and exhibitions at galleries and museums throughout the USA. Her work has been the subject of, or cited in, dozens of articles, books and other publications.[5]

I first met Cynthia in 1997 at an exhibition of jewellery by Flora Book (q.v.) at Mobilia Gallery in Cambridge, Massachusetts. She was kind enough to show me some strikingly beautiful spoons of simple but ingenious design that she had made. I knew immediately that I would want a piece from her. To satisfy herself that her creation was truly functional, she served her family lasagne with it before cleaning it and sending it off to me.

Pudding slice

Sterling silver

Lexington, Massachusetts, 1997

Length 14 ³⁄₈ in. (36.5 cm)

Weight 12.5 oz (388 g)

Cake slice
Sterling silver
Oxford, Ohio, 1994
Length 13 ½ in. (34.5 cm)
Weight 10.4 oz (323 g)

Susan Ewing

The blade has been made as if from a segment of a circular carborundum-toothed saw-blade: a suitably notched sheet of fourteen-gauge silver has been folded back on itself to produce a sandwich of which the top surface does not completely cover the bottom. The turned crease has been chamfered to made a dull cutting edge. The bottom surface of the blade is pierced with an off-centre hole, and the top with a peripheral key shape. The cutting edge is approximately 5 ⅞ in. (15 cm) long. The blade is polished on the exterior surfaces and the interior has a white pickle finish. The handle is a curved eighteen-gauge (1 mm) tube that is attached off-centre to the rear of the bottom plate. It has a sand-blasted spiral along its length and terminates in a 6 ⅝ in. (17 cm) diameter, eighteen-gauge circular-saw finial that has a whited finish and is part creased upwards out of the plane. A short bandsaw segment attaches at the finial and carries a small charm – a cast hand!

Obviously, function yielded to form in this *ex voto* work, since this sculptural tribute may be used only upon danger of self-inflicted bodily harm. The server owes nothing to stylistic history and emphasizes the independence and originality of the artist. Mechanization takes command in this very individual and personal interpretation. This object is active, not passive. It is an instrument. It demands attention. The serrated wheel and blade give visual warnings to the inattentive. In its humour, its startling form and its reassessment of design this is a truly Post-Modern piece.

Artist's philosophy/statement: "Through my pieces designed for use … I am demonstrating that the object cannot be defined or constrained strictly by its function. I use function in terms of the typology of the form, as it is but one of the elements to be considered in the final aesthetic and conceptual solution. I am most concerned with inventing and animating abstract forms while working with pure shapes and volumes. The use of the *ex voto* as a conceptual element was inspired by the myriad of *ex votos* I have encountered in the chapels of the cathedrals and churches visited during my travels. … My votive forms are dedicated to the patron saint of metalsmiths, St Eligius, for sparing my left hand, which I cut severely in 1981 in a bandsaw accident. … This new series remains true to my earlier works, with geometric shapes dealt with structurally, architecturally, as the predominant visual element. … I am most interested in exploring the notion of rotation which results simply through the positive/negative shapes within the edges."

Born: Lawrenceville, Illinois, 1955
Training and work: Stephens College, Columbia, MO, associated arts (music), 1975; Indiana University, BA jewellery design and metalsmithing, 1977; MFA, 1980; study with Aldo Vitali, Rome, 1987. Associate instructor, Indiana University, 1978–80; visiting assistant professor, Miami University, Oxford, OH, 1981–83; jewellery designer, Luxembourg, 1983–84; professor, Miami University, 1984– ; principal, Interalia Design, Oxford, OH, 1984– ; visiting faculty, Rochester Institute of Technology, NY, 1988; director, Miami University International Summer Jewellery Workshop, Rome, 1990.

Artist in residence, Art Park, Lewiston, NY, 1985. Over a dozen prizes and awards for excellence and distinction, and many grants in support of teaching, research and artistic accomplishment. Dozens of invited lectures and workshops at various institutions and art centres. Dozens of citations and articles on her work in newspapers and craft magazines, including television coverage.[6] Membership of and offices in numerous professional organizations. Service as juror, panellist and curator. Several one-person exhibitions in USA and Europe and innumerable exhibitions and competitions. Her work is in many collections, including those of the White House, museums and private collectors.

In agreeing to a schedule for delivery of the server, Susan and I planned nine months ahead, to my seventy-fifth birthday. Imagine my surprise when a large poppy-seed cake arrived with the implement. Needless to say, this was the server that I used (with great care) to cut her gracious gift.

Robert Farrell

The blade has something of a long oval character. It is asymmetric and is split into lesser and major parts. The lesser part attaches to a cylindrical sterling part-handle. The major part attaches to a larger mixed-metal cylinder that portrays a beach scene at Casey Key, Florida: copper sand with black *shakudo* palm-tree trunks and *shibuichi* fronds; the ocean water is nickel silver; and the sun is 18k gold with a sterling-silver sky. Although formally a fish server, it will obviously do quite well for cake – an illustration of the often semantic and artificial nature of the separation of server function into categories.

Blade and handle of this article are creative innovations that work very well. This object combines simplicity of line, complex ornamentation and a new approach to form in the split blade. Farrell has chosen not to be literal in his design source, eschewing fish, fins and wave forms for a landlubber's view of the coast that is kept to a 'narrative' section of the handle. This is a refreshingly original piece that confronts the functional brief with great success, while incorporating a very personal perspective.

Artist's philosophy/statement: "The ceremonial and ritualistic connotations of serving implements, the elegance of simplicity, and the inherent usefulness of an object are three ideas that form the basis of the majority of my work. The fish server evolved from these fundamental prerequisites. While the ceremonial allusions and simplicity of design come naturally and unconsciously to my work, the utility of a piece, including that of the fish server, is often where the challenge must be met. What I hope to have created in this fish server is a twentieth-century artefact. My work stubbornly confronts our world of plastic and polyester throwaways. From a design standpoint, my views are quite simple. I find more grace and elegance in a single line with the right curve to it than in a mass of the most intricate filigree. When asked to create a fish server, my first reaction was to depict fish. While I find a great deal of beauty in animal life, I find even more beauty in earth, its varied formations, and its varied plantlife. Thus, for this project, I chose not to depict fish themselves, but their habitat. As I do not live in, nor on, water, my view of the sea is its shoreline and all of the beauty inherent in any spot where land meets water. The challenge in every piece that I make, as in this fish server, is to integrate function and vision."

Born: Fort Atkinson, Wisconsin, 1960

Training and work: University of Wisconsin, Whitewater, BA English, 1987, BA studio art, 1987; Tyler School of Art, MFA, 1989. Instructor and part-time faculty, Tyler School of Art, 1989–90; assistant, Haystack Mountain, 1990. Lectured at a number of teaching institutions.

First place, Wisconsin Collegiate Showcase, 1986; award of excellence, Lakefront Festival of Arts, Milwaukee Art Museum, 1986–87, 1990–92; fellowship, Tyler School of Art, 1988; scholarship, Haystack Mountain, 1990; award, Crafts National, Pennsylvania State University, 1990; first and second place awards, Cherry Creek Arts Festival, 1991 and 1992; first place and award of excellence, Midwest Salute to the Masters, Fairview Heights, IL, 1991 and 1992; award of excellence, Coconut Grove Festival of Arts, FL, 1992. Numerous juried and invitational gallery and museum exhibitions. Various articles on his work in newspapers and national craft magazines. Farrell's work is in the collection of the American Craft Museum, NY, and several other galleries.[7]

I have never met Robert; his work became known to me through published examples in various craft magazines. We spoke many times by telephone. His zeal and enthusiasm match his creativity. I was quite taken with the designs that he forwarded.

Fish slice

Blade of sterling silver,

handle of sterling and mixed metals

Fort Atkinson, Wisconsin, 1993

Length 12 ¾ in. (32.5 cm)

Total weight 10.8 oz (337 g); silver 9.2 oz (286 g)

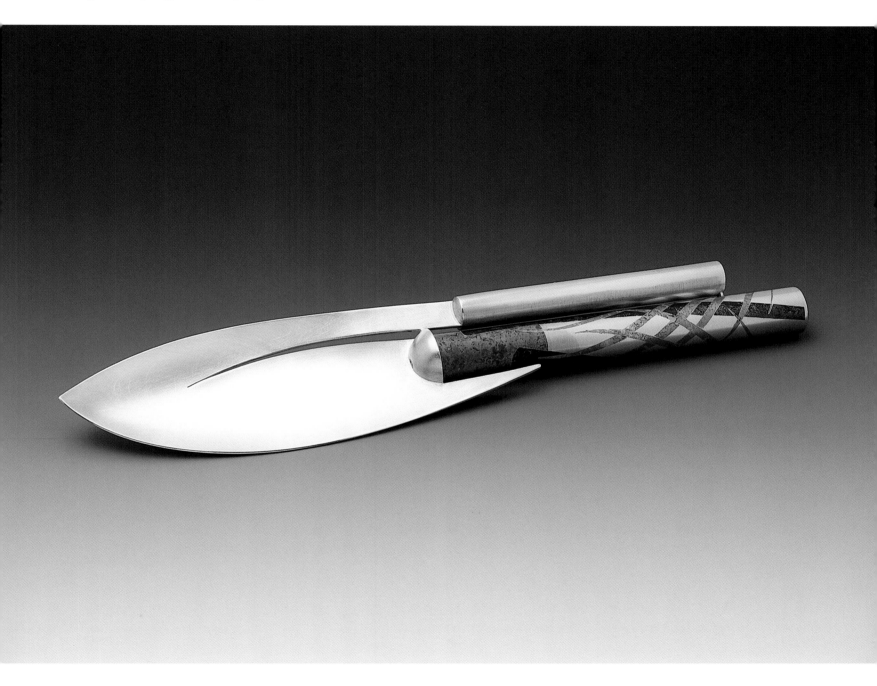

William Frederick

The server blade has the shape of a round-shouldered trowel. The flat forged handle is attached to a wide rear apron that provides lift. The handle carries an applied pierced finial decoration that echoes the blade shape. The latter is pierced in an ingenious oval pattern with repetition of the word *FISH*, which also reads when the server is turned over. The blade is bevelled on all of its edges. The server has a polished finish.

This is a latter-day version of an eighteenth-century Continental-style trowel of the simple undecorated so-called Queen Anne style. In this server, Frederick has played with the contrast of starkly simple form and outline and detailed pierced ornament. While the surface recalls the simplicity of early eighteenth-century English silver, the formal lettered piercing is very Art Deco. The handle is almost spanner-like in its finial shape, suggesting that this is a serviceable and sensible tool for serving, appropriating mass-produced metaphors for a luxury object.

Artist's philosophy/statement: "My approach to design is that followed by industrial designers whereby the client almost invariably places some limits on the design range – financial, functional *etc*. The challenge becomes one of accepting the opportunity to design within the set limits … to produce a solution with artistic quality. One strives to make a technically perfect product using only hand tools, in this case, those originally belonging to the Chicago Kalo Shop. … The overall silhouette of the fish server is intended to recall fish forms generally. The thrust of the pierced teardrop design is to make a contemporary statement by using the letters of the alphabet as abstract design motifs so as to function as a textured area. The mirror image therein further contributes to that effect, while on the reverse side of the server that portion reads as standard lettering."

Born: Sycamore, Illinois, 1921

Training and work: Gallager School of Business, Dip. Bus. Admin., 1939–41; Harvard University, 1942–43; Mass. Instit. Tech. BS, 1946; School of Art, Institute of Chicago, BFA, 1953; MFA, 1959; School for American Craftsmen, Rochester, NY, 1958. Established workshop in 1960 in Chicago. He has taught, particularly metalsmithing and design, at a number of institutions, including the school of the Art Institute of Chicago, 1954–60; Loyola University, Chicago, 1974–78; Columbia College, Chicago, 1976–77.

Sterling Silversmiths Guild of America Medal, 1958; Silversmithing Award, Wichita Art Association, 1960; Father Totte Memorial Award, Religious Art Exhibition, Detroit, 1964; merit award, the Goldsmith Exhibition, Renwick Gallery, Washington, and Minnesota Museum of Art, 1974. Many one-man and group exhibitions, juried and invitational, at museums, galleries and universities, including: Art Institute of Chicago; Dallas Museum of Fine Arts; Renwick Gallery, Washington; Minnesota Museum of Art; and University of Arizona.

I had the pleasure of meeting Bill when he attended the opening of the server exhibition at Goldsmiths' Hall, London. He was one of a small group of US silversmiths that was able to be there. He is a valuable connection with the immediate post-Second World War period.

Fish slice

Sterling silver

Chicago, Illinois, 1993

Length 13 ¾ in. (35 cm)

Weight 13.2 oz (410 g)

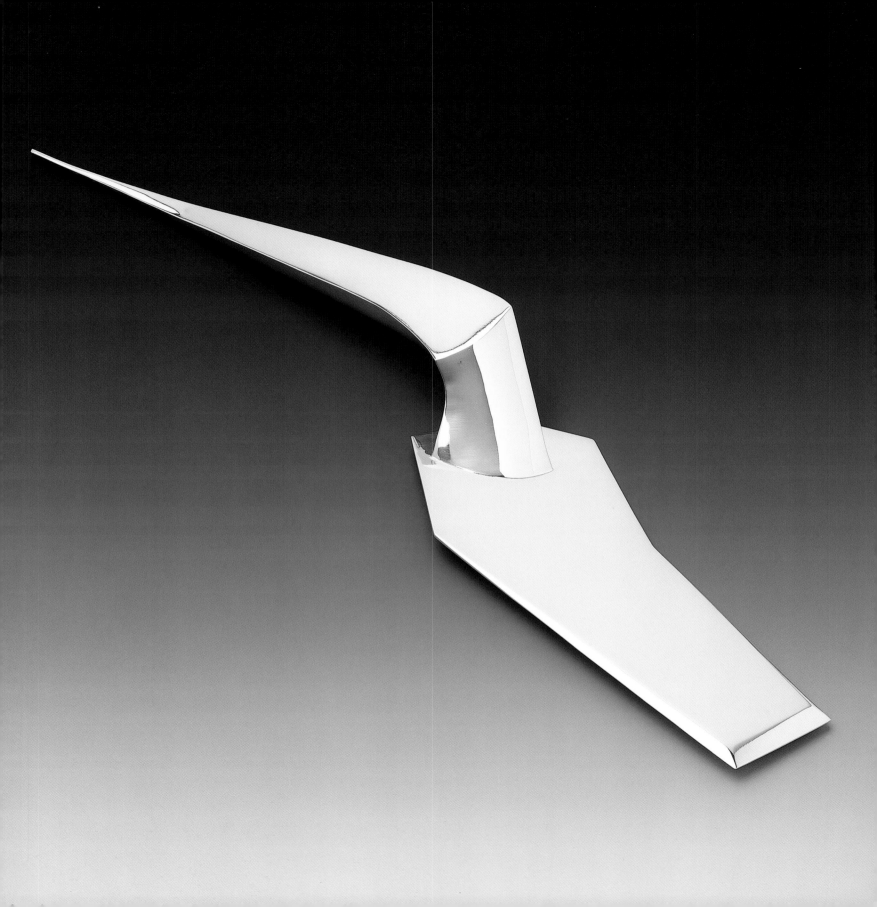

Server
Sterling silver
Seattle, Washington, 1998
Length 17 ⅝ in. (45 cm)
Weight 10.9 oz (339 g)

David Gackenbach

The heptagonal, angular, fourteen-gauge blade is derived from a spatular form. The broad flat end can only lift, or enter a rectangular shaped pan. The blade is bevelled on three leading edges. The hollow handle is made of eighteen-gauge sheet in three sections and with an anticlastic under-section. Its angular shape complements the blade. The handle cross-section diminishes constantly to the rear and the long taper seems just to miss dwindling to a line. The implement is highly polished on all surfaces.

Gackenbach's solution to the challenge of designing a server centres on the exciting transition from two to three dimensions. His sheets of immaculately flat, highly polished silver remind one of paper, folded origami-style, that rise up into three-dimensional form-filling space with simplicity and boldness. A high level of technical skill and mastery of material is required to make this crisp and effective statement in silver. Apparent simplicity is achieved through confident handling of the metal.

Artist's philosophy/statement: "My work … is a meeting-point of man and material; the intersection of the cultural and the natural. The working of metal is a continual dialogue between maker and material, with the resultant object a balance between what the artist wants and what the material will allow. My pieces exist in a space overlapped by man and nature – a study of the intimacy of the individual life within the space and time of the earth."

Born: Abington, Pennsylvania, 1971
Training and work: Pennsylvania State University, Integrative Arts, BA, 1993; student at Pratt Art Center, Seattle, 1995; University of Washington, metal design, MFA, 1998; Université Franche-Comté, Besançon, France, 1993. Talisman Metal Craft, Seattle, 1994–97. Fabricator, US Starcraft Corporation, Seattle, 1998– ; graduate assistant, University of Washington, 1996–98. Has given and organized several workshops at Pratt and Highline Community College. Consultant, Salishan Public Art Project, 1997. Member of SNAG,

American Craft Council, Seattle Metals Guild.

Third prize, National Student Sterling Design Competition, 1994; Pratt Art Center, C. Anders Memorial Scholarship, 1995; Allied Arts, MFA scholarship and exhibition, 1997; Marsh scholarship and a special projects scholarship, University of Washington, 1997; Thesis exhibition; various US gallery and craft exhibitions. Collection of Coeur d'Alene Mines Corporation; private commissions.

While David was a graduate student in the Art School of the University of Washington, I had ample opportunity to get to know him and to admire the large sculptural copper pieces on which he toiled. I decided that I would like to have him make a server for me. I had previously seen a striking fish slice of his own design – a family gift.

Skip Gaynard

The server is of trowel shape with a pronouncedly asymmetric form. It is bevelled on the left edges and elongated at the right tip and left rear so as to provide the possibility of different useful functions. The boss and stem lift are forged and attach along the rear right under-edge of the blade. The handle is blue dyed and is starred with silver dots; it is held in a conical ferrule and end cap. The former attaches to the lift, and the latter to an irregular, rectangular, two-faced finial piece, each on a short square shaft.

This server is indeed eminently functional, but most striking in its introduction of the dramatic impact of colour on silver. The blue handle, studded piqué-style with silver stars, makes this very bold piece also quite ethereal. The asymmetry of the blade gives this server a very contemporary feeling.

Artist's philosophy/statement: "My continued involvement in ... silversmithing stems not from the tactile quality that comes with silver but more from the investigation of design forms being expressed through a functional object. ... The medium obviously has a great deal to do with how those forms are represented, mainly in the reflective quality of the silver, but in addition, the functionality of utilitarian table-top items dictates a parameter ... that I find interesting in the problem-solving process. Hopefully the solution becomes a harmonious bridge to the issues of form and function."

Born: Visalia, California, 1955

Training and work: California State University, Fresno, BA, 1978; MA, 1980; University of Washington, MFA, 1982. Various specialized workshops. Established Skip Gaynard Designs in 1982 in Fresno; instructor at CSU, Fresno, 1983–85. Inter-media artworks and consultation nationally and internationally. Gaynard is also a musician and composer.

Ford Foundation Award of Merit, 1980; Best-in-the-West Graphics Design Award, 1988; City of Fresno Arts grant, 1988; Los Angeles Collaborative Arts Project, 1988; Golden Oak Awards in Graphic Design, 1989, 1990; guest artist, Kansas State University, 1990; Medical Media Award of Excellence, 1991; Print Design Annual Certificate of Design Excellence, 1992. Many music and metalwork commissions, including six chalices for the use of Pope John Paul II, a presentation piece for Mikhail Barishnikov, and the mace for Eastern Washington University. Numerous one-man and group exhibitions at museums, galleries and universities throughout the USA.

Skip was a graduate student in the metalsmithing studio at the University of Washington when I first began to devote some spare time to beating on silver in earnest. He was accomplished beyond his years and experience. I remember vividly an occasion when he illustrated, in the process of restoring the shape of a bowl with a few deft touches, a maxim expounded by our mutual mentor, John Marshall (q.v.), namely that the best tools we have are our fingers.

Cake slice

Blade of sterling silver, handle of Delrin,

with sterling boss, stem, ferrule, cap and finial

Fresno, California, 1995

Length 12 ¼ in. (31 cm)

Total weight 7.4 oz (230 g)

Fish slice

The blade of sterling and handle of silver-copper *mokumé gané*

Seattle, Washington, 1991

Length 13 in. (33 cm)

Total weight 14.2 oz (442 g)

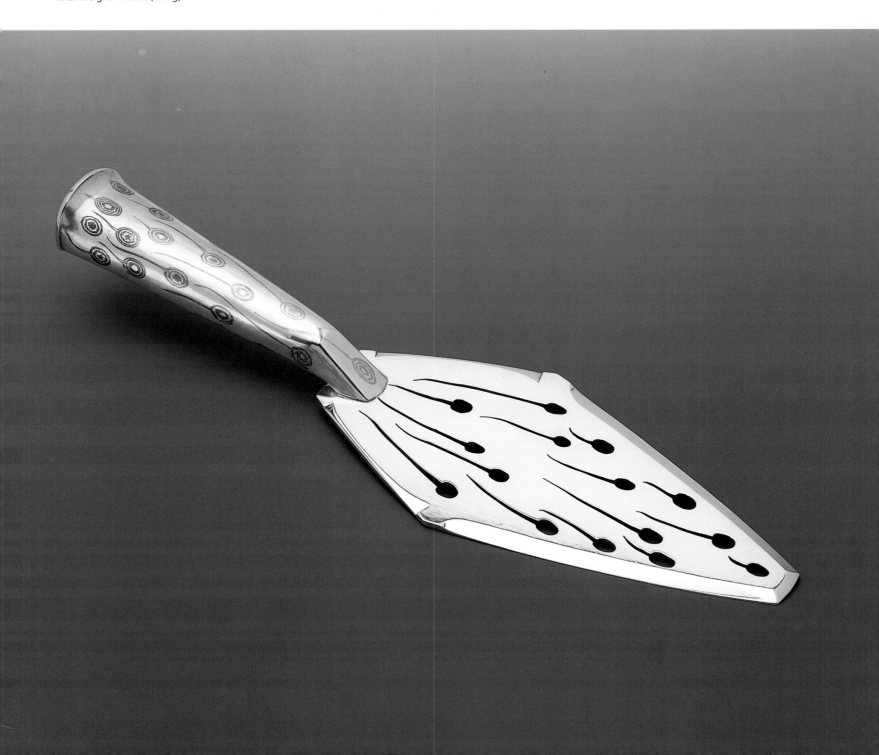

Roger Horner

The blade shape is an *art moderne* version of the old trowel. The striking *mokumé gané* silver-copper material of the handle is derived from its Japanese heritage. This is an elemental object whose bold form and functional handle and blade compound the basic elements of life as its source of inspiration and decoration. This server is a celebration of life itself. Handle and blade are thematically joined as *mokumé gané* spermatozoa wriggle on the pierced blade and become fretted patterns that are at once decorative and functional. This is very much a contemporary and innovative response to the design brief in its direct depiction of life form, on what is nominally a mundane object.

The heavy blade is of a severely geometric trowel shape with four straight-sided lateral components, a flat front edge and heavily bevelled edges. It is pierced with a spermatozoa design. The rounded handle, which lifts from the blade without stem or bolster, is artfully constructed of silver-copper *mokumé gané* and worked so that, by dimpling and filing, a matching blade design has been produced. Engraved *In the beginning* at the end of the handle and *for BSR* underneath.

Artist's philosophy/statement: "I wanted something special for this work. The swimming things in [other] designs caused me to think about how basic swimming is to creation. The design was simply born from those thoughts. We all begin by swimming."

Born: Pasco, Washington, 1934
Training and work: University of Washington, Seattle, BA, 1955, BFA, 1983, MFA, 1986. Technician, University of Washington, 1985–. Retired as colonel in the Pacific Command, US Infantry, Hawaii, in 1979.

Various exhibitions at galleries and museums, nationally and locally. Many commissions for individuals and churches.

Roger, who runs the University of Washington metalwork studio, is a lecturer and always a patient instructor of students in the shop. He gives confidence and guidance to all alike – including the writer, who is delighted to be his friend. His self-made tools are themselves works of art.

Val Link

Fish slice
Sterling silver
Houston, Texas, 1995
Length 14 ¼ in. (36 cm)
Weight 10.8 oz (336 g)

The blade is of triangular shape, orientated to a saw-tooth tip at the left side; it has a swept-up-and-over curve along the right edge, in a wave/surf form. The up-sweep is brightly peened, but the top and bottom of the blade are polished sixteen-gauge sheet and are chisel-engraved with a fleeing school of fish. The handle is a realistic shell-formed shark whose mouth is half buried in the rolling wave. The dorsal and two side fins are cast and soldered to the body. This is an old technique given new life in the USA by Heikki Seppa (q.v.). It is made of eighteen-gauge sheet and has an almost invisible seam along the belly. The fins are added to the bottom. It is quite comfortable in the hand.

This novel server has a very dramatic presence. It is a startling and attention-grabbing design, the shark handle creating a rather menacing image. Link has provided a piece of sculpture as well as a highly functional piece of serving equipment. Perhaps this server could be connected with the zoomorphic forms that are popular within high design produced by such firms as Alessi? The impact of the piece is created through a combination of instant recognition, anxiety and delight. Link has resolved the problem of attaching handle to blade in a very innovative way, uniting them in the body of the shark.

Artist's philosophy/statement: "I would describe my work as sculptured simplicity. … I demand of myself technical precision as well as aesthetic and functional innovation. … In my design I draw creative inspiration from nature as well as man-made form. … I find functionalism to be an intriguing rather than burdensome aspect of creativity and problem solving. Perhaps my greatest pleasure … is the experience of making the purely aesthetic, functional and technical aspects of design composition complement each other and work as one."

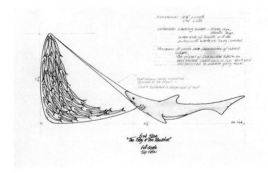

Born: Shreveport, Louisiana, 1940

Training and work: Del Mar Junior College, Corpus Christi, associate of art, 1963; University of Texas, Austin, BFA, 1965; Cranbrook Academy of Art, MI, MFA, 1967. Head, metal-smithing department, Interlochen Arts Academy, MI, 1967–70; designer for Aubergine Inc., Houston, 1988–91; associate professor, University of Houston, 1970– ; self-employed designer-metalsmith, 1970– . Various teaching and work-shop activities.

Master Teaching Award, University of Houston, 1986. Member, American Craft Council, Sterling Silversmiths Guild of America, SNAG. Link has participated in over one hundred and fifty regional, national and international exhibitions. He has published and been the subject of various articles and book chapters. He is an acknowledged expert on hydraulic press forming.[8]

Val first became known to me as the remarkable mentor of two successive First Prize Flatware winners in the Annual National Student Silversmithing Competition – a very considerable tribute to his technical and teaching capabilities. Our acquaintance was improved by his attendance at the opening of the exhibition of the collection at the National Ornamental Metals Museum in Memphis in 1995 and the SNAG conference in Seattle in 1998.

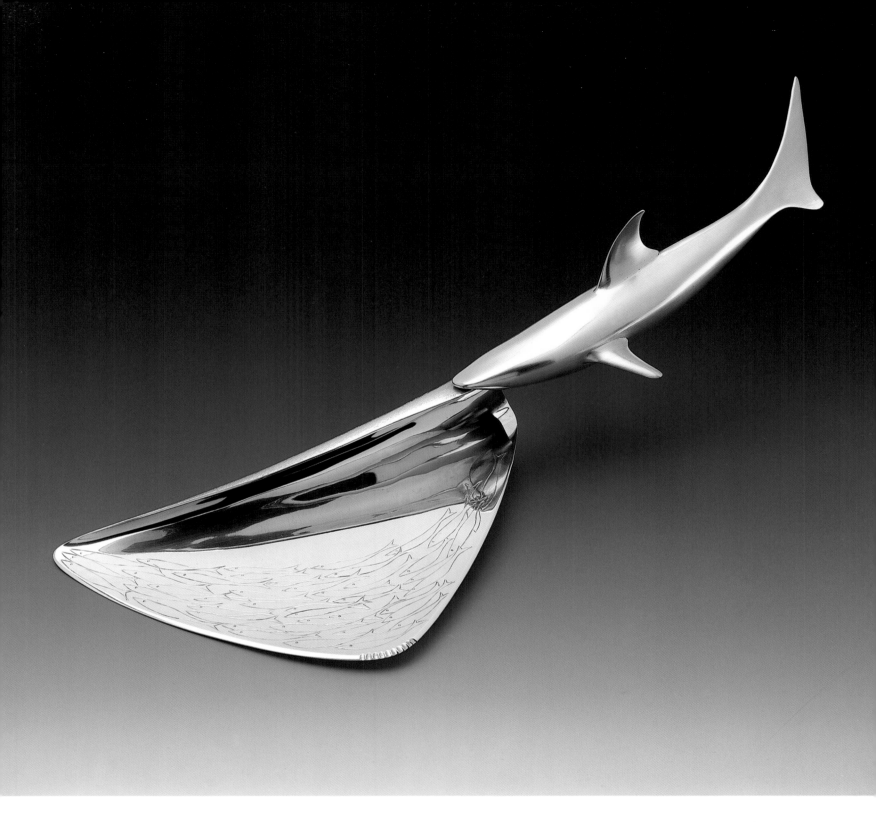

John Marshall

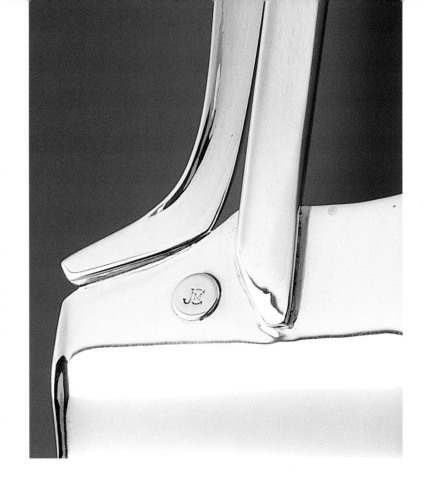

The forged, unpierced blade is a late nineteenth-century cake form. It has a raised apron, to the edge of which is attached a long, split, forged handle. The handle pair is flattened somewhat to make a hand-grip and terminates in two waved, gold trailing-pieces. The bio-organic sentiment of the handle supports the artist's designation of this article as a fish slice, notwithstanding the blade shape.

This server connects with Art Nouveau in the whiplash line of the handle. The design seems to capture a sea creature just about to dart away with a flick of its tail, to disappear under the safety of a rock or a dinner plate. The handle invites one to grasp it before it wriggles away. It is light and delicate in form, yet sturdy in construction. The ornament is integral to the form; shape and decoration are one.

Artist's philosophy/statement: "Function is an integral part of each piece I do – all parts must work within the design and not in conflict with the sculptural movement. I find myself working more conceptually now and [am] less involved with the craft, confident that my hands will perform as a craftsman."

Born: Pittsburgh, Pennsylvania, 1936

Training and work: Cleveland Institute of Art, BFA, 1965; Syracuse University, MFA, 1967. Instructor and assistant professor, Syracuse University, 1965–70; School of Art, University of Washington, Seattle, 1970– , to rank of professor and chairman, metalwork. Has invented or used a number of original techniques such as pressure-forming and *mokumé gané*. Founding member of SNAG and several other societies. He has lectured, juried and published extensively.

Horace C. Potter Award for excellence in silversmithing, Cleveland, 1964; first place award, *Sterling Today*, 1964; second place award, 1965; national merit award, American Craft Council, 1966; Thomas C. Thompson Prize for Enamel, Everson Museum of Art, Syracuse, 1968; Women's Council Award, Rochester, 1969; American Metalcraft Award, St Louis, 1970; second prize, metalwork, 22nd National Decorative Arts Exhibition, Wichita, 1972; honour award, Friends of Craft, Seattle, 1973; gold medal award, Academia Italiana delle Arte e del Lavoro, Parma, 1981; named to College of Fellows, American Craft Council, 1993. Innumerable one-man shows and exhibitions world-wide, including a retrospective exhibition at the National Ornamental Metals Museum, Memphis, 1991. His work is in many international museums. Commissions include private individuals, public bodies and foundations.[9]

I met John in 1978 after I returned from sabbatical in London, where I had had a brief introduction to silversmithing at the Sir John Cass School of Art. I was delighted to learn that my own university had a metalwork studio and that the head of the programme was an outstanding smith. Our acquaintance progressed to friendship. John graciously allowed me to use a bench and to listen to his instruction as I hovered around the circle of students who watched his demonstrations of technique. I decided to make my articles very heavy – not to last through centuries or to proclaim quality, but so that I had enough material in reserve to be able to file away my mistakes!

Server

Sterling silver with 14k gold

Seattle, Washington, 1990

Length 19½ in. (49.5 cm)

Weight 12.4 oz (386 g)

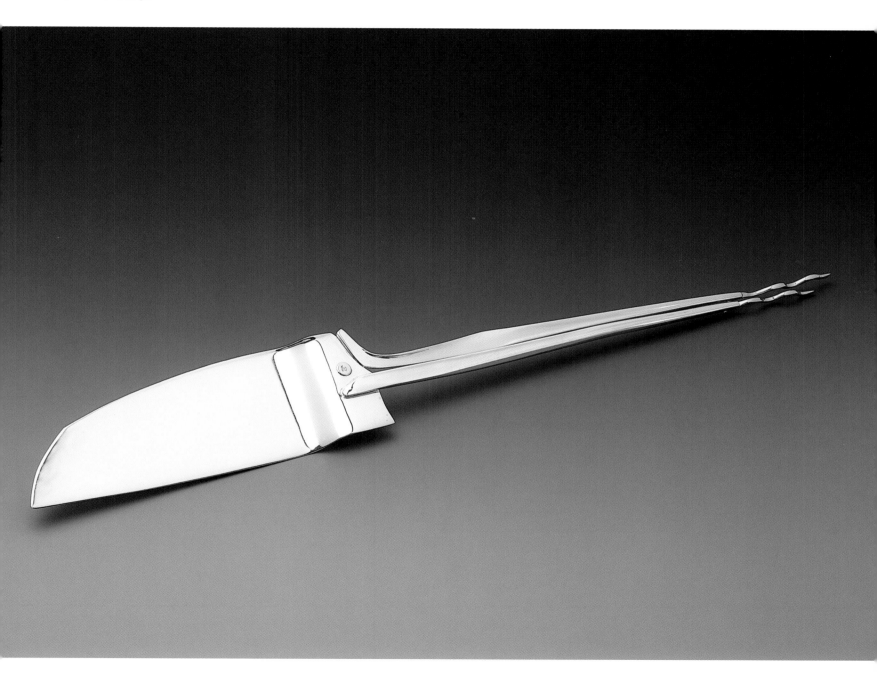

Kurt Matzdorf

The bevelled blade is of asymmetric trowel shape with a truncated slanted front edge. It is engraved and pierced with fish forms that are threatened by a voracious pursuer. The heavy handle is carried by a large, vertical, concave, bolster-apron lift at the rear of the blade. It has a roller-imprinted cloth pattern topside and a polished multiple-finger grip on its underside. A large script *R* has been applied to the butt end as a personal touch (for the commissioner).

This implement is a modern version of the eighteenth-century trowel. The asymmetric blade adds delightful novelty while the heavy lift and handle confer solidity and utility. This is a supremely functional piece with a bold grip-handle and generous blade. It sits firmly in the hand, and pushes neatly and firmly under the fish. There is no doubt, of course, that this is for fish, and for eating, as the open mouths of men and fish race off the blade. It is an open, honest piece that captures the maker's sense of fun. It is personal yet timeless in its design.

Artist's philosophy/statement: "When I entered the contemporary silversmithing scene in 1953, it appeared to me to be almost a wasteland. I resolved to make it a fun and meaningful art once again. The field of ceremonial and religious silver-smithing seemed to be particularly well suited to the storytelling that I enjoy and the creation of beauty to which I wanted to dedicate my life. ... As to my own style: a friend who is very active and knowledgeable in the crafts described it as contemporary 'classic'. That suits me just fine!"

Born: Stadtoldendorf, Germany, 1922

Training and work: London University, Diploma in Fine Art (sculpture), 1949, and private study in Oxford with sculptor Benno Elkan; University of Iowa, MFA silversmithing, 1954. Faculty, State University of New York, New Paltz, 1957–85; presently founding professor emeritus of gold and silver-smithing.

College of Fellows of American Craft Council; founding member and board director, SNAG, 1970–75. Numerous awards and prizes, one-man exhibitions, international exhibitions and over one hundred national invitational exhibitions. Work in permanent collections of several museums, including: New York State Museum; Jewish Museum, New York; and Minnesota Museum of Art. Innumerable commissions – awards, trophies, maces, chains of office and medallions – for government, universities, institutions, synagogues and private individuals. Has been juror for national design competitions; consultant, visiting lecturer at American and foreign universities. He is widely known for his ceremonial and religious works.

I knew Kurt first only by reputation and through our several telephone conversations and various articles that had appeared concerning him and his work. It was a pleasure later to visit him and his wife, Alice, in their home in New Paltz and to see his remarkably compact, well-equipped workshop and to have a personal exposition of his many commissions.

Fish slice

Sterling silver

New Paltz, New York, 1991

Length 13 ⅜ in. (34 cm)

Total weight 16 oz (496 g)

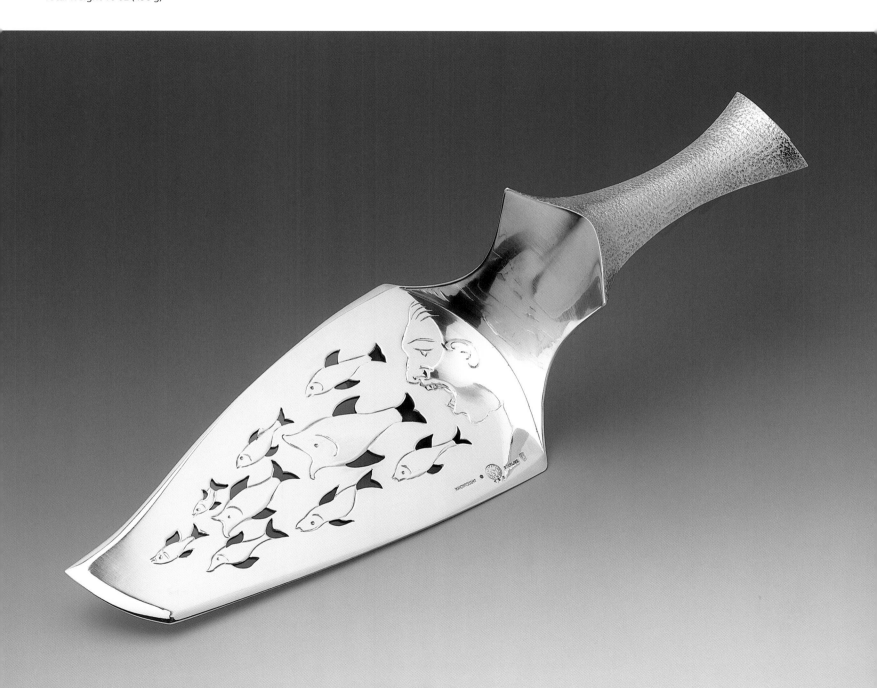

Komelia Hongja Okim

Server
Sterling silver, fine gold
Rockville, Maryland, 1999
Length 12 in. (30.5 cm)
Weight 15.2 oz (472 g)

The server has the form of a human figure. The blade (head) is a transverse navette shape, the leading edge of which is sharpened and presents an undulating waved or scalloped contour. Its surface has a scoured finish. The blade attaches by an underpiece to a complex handle-frame made from oxidized, vertical, silver bands of variable width (roughly 1 cm) and thickness (approximately 1–1.6 mm). The handle has the overall shape of the torso, with outstretched arms and a complex anatomy made up of curves, scallops and angular shapes. The structure is highlighted by five small circles and arched areas with textured goldfoil surfaces applied by burnishing, a Korean technique called *kum-boo*.[10]

Okim has used the opportunity of this commission to create a striking decorative extravaganza. The solid, flat and matte navette blade makes a bold contrast to the structure of the handle. Silver is used in flat strip almost like Victorian scrolled paper work, called quilling, to create a light but detailed pattern, reminiscent of the Jazz Age. Alternating curve and right-angle also suggests scale and fin, and perhaps the rapid swish of some marine animal. The gilded finial and detailing add a sense of glamour and luxury.

Artist's philosophy/statement: "… I interweave my cultural heritage into artistic creations. Attempting to integrate Korean and contemporary Western techniques, I envision a dynamic contrast in which differing elements unite to produce natural harmony. My work depicts the relationship between people and landscapes, symbolizing the gestures and moods of humans in their natural environment. Further, it reflects the principles of feng shui, a philosophy focused on the relationship between humans and their environment. I design artworks which express aesthetic integrity and functional values. My objective is to combine traditional Korean and American surface embellishment techniques on metal. I focus on balancing my media, materials and colours. Their philosophical basis touches upon the Taoist principles of nature, including the yin-yang theory, dual system and vital energy of the life force, as well as the cosmic environment."

Born: Korea, 1939

Training and work: Ewha Women's University, Seoul, fibre arts, 1958–61; Indiana University, metal arts, BA, 1969, MFA, 1973. Department of Arts, Montgomery College, Rockville, MD, 1972– , presently professor. Fulbright Exchange scholar, Hong-Ik University, Korea, 1982–83, and Wo-Kwange University, Korea, 1994–95; visiting exchange professor, University of Wisconsin, Madison, 1985–86. Since 1981 she has given over eighty workshops and lectures in the USA, Norway, Russia and Korea at colleges and summer institutes. Okim is a distinguished member of SNAG and is active in a number of American–Korean artists' associations. She is the USA correspondent for *Korean Craft Art Magazine* and is currently president of the Ewha Woman's University Metal Arts Association.

Okim has had many one-person and group invitational exhibitions and has received several prizes, merit awards and special recognition. Her life as teacher, mother and artist has been the subject of a travelling video. Her research on patination has been supported by a Montgomery County Arts Council grant. Her work is in several museums and public sites in the USA and Korea and has been shown in various travelling exhibitions.

I met Komelia at the SNAG National Conference in Seattle in March 1998. I had earlier been impressed by a strong and dramatic teapot by her that was on exhibition at the Seafirst Gallery, in a display curated by Marilyn and Jack da Silva. Following strong endorsement by Chunghi Choo (q.v.), we met over a cup of coffee and concluded an agreement.

Server

Sterling silver

Deer Isle, Maine, 1993

Length 14 in. (35.5 cm)

Weight 11.7 oz (365 g)

Ronald Pearson

This implement may function easily as either a fish, cake or pastry server. The triangular blade is a very slightly dished sheet and is pierced with a curving wave shape along its centre length. The forged handle was made by an old blacksmithing technique: a reverse twist – one and a half turns right, forge, three-quarter turn left – in this case, producing a spiral of oval flats. The handle joins the blade with a top-side rat-tail junction. The blade is polished and the handle has a butler finish.

This server was designed for function and is enhanced by its forged handle. The ripple effect relates to the work of the English silversmiths Toby Russell and Alex Brogden (q.v.), who also relish the malleability of the metal, which lends itself to this wave-like treatment and exploits the reflective quality of silver. The ripples in Pearson's handle are echoed in the fretted ripples in the blade, creating a sort of positive/negative effect and uniting both parts of the server. The simplicity of the design belies Pearson's mastery over the material, and the delicacy of his workmanship.

Artist's philosophy/statement: "The hammer is our primary tool. In skilled hands, it will shape malleable metal into simple or complex fluid forms. … It is the challenge to explore new terrain that makes this work so exciting." Arline Fisch adds: "The forms evolve from his direct manipulation of the metal … as a totally plastic material which can be stretched and compressed into graceful lines and planes in space. He produces flowing organic shapes." His work "displays the beauty of forged silver, with its rapid change of plane, the tension of the tapered line, the gentle curve of an edge, the soft reflections of the surface".[11]

Born: New York, 1924 **Died**: 1996
Training and work: University of Wisconsin, 1942–43; Alfred University School for American Craftsmen, 1947–48; Reed and Barton special design program, 1949. First workshop concentrated on spun-bronze hollowware, 1948; moved on to production jewellery, 1950. Co-founding craftsman of Shop One, Rochester, NY, 1952–76; started blacksmithing and iron work, 1966; moved workshops to Deer Isle, ME, 1971. For over thirty years designer and consultant to numerous commercial firms, including Hickok Jewelry Company, David Morgan Ltd, Kirk-Stieff Company and Dansk International. Founding member of SNAG. Lectured and conducted workshops at a number of academic institutions and schools of craft, including Haystack Mountain and Penland.

Many prizes and honourable mentions in exhibitions throughout the country from 1948. Acted as a consultant to and board member, trustee or director of many governmental and private programmes and organizations. Exhibited world-wide in innumerable exhibitions. Commissioned by prestigious institutions such as Harvard University, Massachusetts Institute of Technology, Minnesota Museum of Art, Smithsonian Institution and many others, and by private individuals. Both the author and subject of many articles in books and magazines.

Ronald was one of the pioneer silversmiths of this era, and his work soon became known to me. Unfortunately, my encounters with him were only indirect, via telephone calls and correspondence. I regret the lost opportunity to know personally this important contributor to the American craft scene, but feel fortunate that he agreed to accept a part in this enterprise.

David Peterson

This article is basically a striking sculptural concept, of limited functional capability. The oval blade is in two parts: an outer segment with a polished surface, and an inner asymmetric oval that is pierced with a raised oval shape and which has a glass-bead-blasted, dull-grey, stone-like surface. The four struts of the handle are held by a vertical oval ring that joins the horizontal flat of the stem. Two copper pins on the inner oval are ornamental. On the underside, three copper pins hold the front end of the vertical strut; another holds the strut at the rear of the inner oval. The underside of the inner oval is chased with a densely stippled surface.

Peterson's sculptural aptitude is very evident in this piece, which is original in concept and design. Form has triumphed over function in this complex and elaborate construction, which questions the relationship between inner and outer spaces. The handle recalls the fossil belemnite form, where the inner body has been replaced with a 'skeleton' of stone. The strength of line and of outline connects this piece with other styles that focus on powerful linear forms. Hence the creator's sympathy with Celtic traditions and Charles Rennie Mackintosh's attenuated rectilinear forms, which were the precursors of the Modern Movement.

Artist's philosophy/statement: "Many of my recent works are concerned with the abstruse and the incongruous. By means of cryptic and complex juxtapositions I hope to evoke a sense of mystery, provoking the viewer to engage in a sort of aesthetic Rorschach Test. … While I do not, consciously, make use of overt historical or stylistic references in my work, I have no doubt that my long love affair with Celtic antiquities has done much to inform and refine my sensibilities. I will also acknowledge that I now see more than a little Mackintosh in the server. … When I think back, I don't recall that I approached the problem of the server differently than I would any other sculptural work. There seems to me no logic, no truth, in distinguishing some creative works, by virtue of their utility, as being outside the *pure realm* of sculpture. Indeed, the elemental form of a server, with its counterposed blade and handle, seems to be a most perfect armature upon which to build a sculpture. The qualities of kinetic movement and tactile interaction, often of key importance to my work, encourage *the viewer* to engage in a haptic, as well as a visual, experience."

Born: Rochester, New York, 1958

Training and work: State University, Genesee, NY, BA, 1980; Indiana State University, Terre Haute, MFA, 1982. Designer and associate art director, Champion Products Inc., 1978–80, 1983–84. Studio artist, goldsmithing and sculpture, 1976– . Assistant professor of art, Purdue University, 1984–89; associate professor of art, Skidmore College, NY, 1989– . Guest lecturer, visiting faculty, juror, visiting curator at museums, workshops and conferences, universities and craft schools.

Benjamin Blumberg travel scholarship, 1981; Purdue University, faculty research grant, 1984; annual fellowship, 1987; SNAG research fellowship, 1986–87; Indiana Arts Commission fellowship, 1989; Skidmore College, faculty research grants, 1991–93. Many one-man and group exhibitions at galleries, colleges and universities in the USA and abroad, with numerous honourable mentions, merit prizes, best-of-show citations *etc*.

I was attracted to David's work by a marvellous spoon he contributed to the Roseanne Raab collection. I finally met David when he visited the exhibition at Goldsmiths' Hall, London, in 1995. He came to dinner and we enjoyed a chat about his background and interests, among other things. We met again at the SNAG conference in Seattle in 1998.

Pastry slice

Sterling silver save for very minor copper construction elements

Saratoga Springs, New York, 1994

Length 12 ⅝ in. (32 cm)

Weight 8.1 oz (253 g)

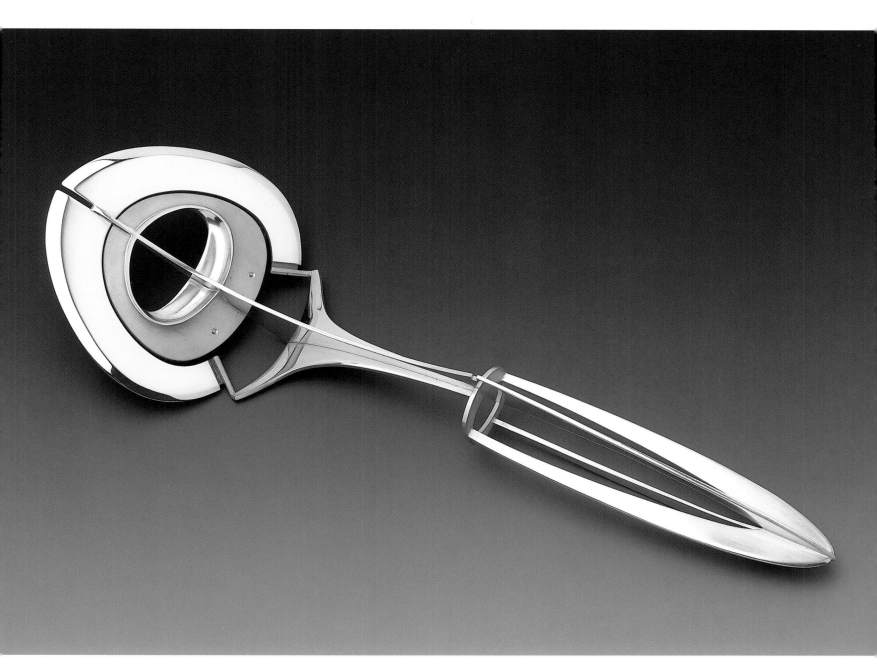

Harold Schremmer

The polished blade is a rounded triangle with up-turned right edge and four upturned, fluted and pointed cusps at the rear of the blade. The blade is pierced with bubbles and turns up with a 1¾ in. (4.5 cm), strengthened, fluted lift and enters the body of a monster fossil fish handle. The head is deeply textured and oxidized and has two features: a bony structure that carries two eyes made of epoxy in which are embedded tiny beads of blue and gold; and a large gilded mouth having a large protruding tongue, and inset with bony lower canines and upper ivory teeth. The head attaches to a two-part, scratch-brushed body-handle with a large fluked tail and down-curving stand. The server is made of thirteen separate parts, held by tiny 4-40 stainless miniature machine bolts. The tongue is secured with three 2-36 bolts. Gold plating is 24k, and is triple plate and scratch-brush burnished between each layer. The teeth are bezel, tab set. The whole server is demountable, if need be.

Schremmer delights in the contrast of colour and texture. Never before has a silversmith been so bold in the choice and treatment of materials. Intricate work-manship and inventive imagination, given freedom, have produced a modern 'grotesque', defined by Peacham in 1612 as "an unnatural or unorderly composition for delight's sake, of men, beasts, birds, fishes, flowers". It combines elements of the Baroque and Arts and Crafts, as well as being undeniably contemporary.

Artist's philosophy/statement: This piece was inspired by a fossil fish found in a slate quarry in Germany. "A major task was how to join the different parts … what would be the order of combination … non-metal parts cannot take the heat of soldering, … gold-plated parts are best removeable. … I've been amazed at the great difference that slight changes in body parts can make … some are more expressive than others. I am especially aware of texture, contrast, line, mass. … This piece went through dozens of patterns, models, test pieces. … Of course the piece must function properly, be comfortable to hold, easy to clean, possible to repair (… if the piece has to be worked on in the next five hundred years) … When you told me to make the server as if it would be my own … that insight into an artists' mind is very rare … was very significant for me."

Born: Hartford, Connecticut, 1928

Training and work: School of Museum of Fine Arts, Boston, BFA, 1953, MA, 1958. Established silversmithing studio in Hartford, CT, 1958–67; freelance design and commissions, emphasizing religious art. Studied in Germany, 1967–70, at the Staatliche Werkunstschule Schwabish Gmünd, and at the Kunst- und Werkschule-Pforzheim. Established studio in Stafford Springs, CT, 1971–73. Instructor and professor, Rhode Island School of Design, 1971–74; Department chairman, jewellery and silversmithing, Portland School of Art, ME, 1978–87. Re-established as self-employed silversmith, West Warwick, RI, 1987– .

School of Museum of Fine Arts, Boston, scholarship, 1949–53; Joslin and Bartlett travelling scholarships, 1953, 1956. First prize, National Silversmithing Competition, Rhode Island, 1962; first prize, Contemporary Liturgical Art, Philadelphia, 1962; L.C. Tiffany Foundation grant, 1963, and travelling scholarship, 1966; School of Museum of Fine Arts, Boston award, 1964; honour award for silversmithing, American Society for Church Architecture, 1965. Active in various offices of Connecticut State Crafts Society. Commissions for St Peter's, Rome; several America's Cup trophies; President's badge of office, Rhode Island School of Design; President's medal, Portland School of Art. Exhibitions of decorative and ecclesiastical art throughout the USA.

Hal and I enjoyed many telephone conversations over a period of two years during the course of this creative experience. The design of the server evolved over a long period. He deeply appreciated the freedom afforded by the mandate, as opposed to many closely defined ecclesiastical commissions that weighed on his artistic aestheticism. He began to bubble as he got into the project, and jokingly threatened to make more servers (ideas that kept coming to his mind) than I had in my whole collection.

Fish slice

Sterling server, ivory and bone, stainless-steel screws and plastic eye

West Warwick, Rhode Island, 1995

Length 15 ½ in. (39.5 cm)

Total weight 21.5 oz (670 g)

Fish slice
Sterling silver
Cleveland, Ohio, 1994
Length 11¾ in. (30 cm)
Weight 10.7 oz (332 g)

Andrea Schweitzer

The blade is a modified, free trowel shape with looping curvilinear undulation. On the rear one-third of the blade there is applied cut-card work, which simulates finger-like seaweed or biomorphic forms creeping over the blade. The blade and cut-card work have different finishes of scratch brushing. The handle is an asymmetric, twisted porpoise tail; the bright pitted surface was applied by a high-speed stone wheel. The underside is acid-etched with scale and marine forms.

The blade of this implement depicts very well the freedom of form that is expressed in many American designs. Schweitzer's server almost swims across the table; it takes the essence of fish-like motion as its form. The serpentine line created by the cast handle runs down through the blade, echoed by the fretted patterns cut into the surface. This object is alive. In its asymmetry and capture of motion, this server takes Rococo principles and applies them to contemporary design.

Artist's philosophy/statement: "I believe that the [design of the] 'business end' of silver serving implements should be very thoughtful so that they work for what they are intended to do. …I try to incorporate those functional elements with whimsical … imagery. This makes these pieces fun, approachable *and* functional. … Silver is a very special metal. To me it is a feminine metal with which I love to work. … I derived the design from various sea creatures. … The handle is a stylized porpoise tail. It was designed to fit comfortably in the right or left hand. … The [sponsor] left the project wide open to my creative interpretation … ."

Born: Indianapolis, Indiana, 1971
Training and work: Cleveland Institute of Art, BFA, 1995; Indiana University teacher certification program, 1995– . Various jewellery workshops and classes. Cleveland Institute of Art scholarships, 1992–93. First place for flatware in National Student Sterling Design competition, 1993. Mary Millkin Art Education scholarship, 1996. Various student exhibitions and Class of '93 Exhibition, Goldsmiths' Hall, London.

Andrea's work came to my attention after she won the flatware prize in the Fortunoff National Student Silverware Competition in 1993. Support of the silversmithing craft is even more gratifying when the commissionee is a person just getting started on what will, we hope, be an outstanding career. In this case, Andrea has developed yet more art forms, namely belly-dancing and costume-making, which were summer activities during her undergraduate studies. She continues in the several areas of her interests.

Heikki Seppa

The blade is trowel-shaped, but the resemblance to a trowel ends there. The triangular blade is grasped at the rear and back right edge by a rising, hollow, curling handle that is very strong by reason of the anticlastic-synclastic bi-shell-forming structure technique pioneered by Seppa. It is surprisingly comfortable in the hand and effective to use.

Seppa developed and reinvigorated this structural technique in the USA. Dozens – probably hundreds – of silversmiths have learned anti- and synclastic raising in workshops he has given all over the country. The simple form he has created is very powerful in its expression. The stark directness of this server seems to relate to a very Scandinavian approach to design, in which the functional gives way to the sculptural if there is an aesthetic advantage to be gained. It is part of the free-form movement begun in the 1950s that combined innovative boldness with conservative tradition. Seppa has handled this brief with characteristic clarity and control, creating organic references through abstract statement.

Artist's philosophy/statement: "In my philosophy, what you say is important – and what you say it with (the medium) must be used to its fullest. The ductility and malleability of metals – silver and gold – are the strongest characteristics through which the smiths can create forms and structures. I believe these to be more profound means to convey expressions and meaning than surface treatments, *i.e.* graphic means." In forming this implement, Seppa intends a deeper meaning: "A celebration – of whatever, from the embryonic tip of the spiral, through the vicissitudes of life – finally one gets to eat cake."

Born: Finland, 1927
Training and work: Goldsmith School of Helsinki, three years; Central School of Industrial Art of Finland, four years; Cranbrook Academy of Art, MI, one year. Workman, Hopeatakomo Oy, Helsinki, 1945–48; Georg Jensen, Copenhagen 1948–49; pipefitter, Columbia Cellulose, BC, Canada, 1951–60; teacher, Art Center, Louisville, KY, 1961–65; professor, Washington University, St Louis, 1965–92; professor emeritus, 1992– . Has conducted dozens of workshops on design and technique at Haystack Mountain, Deer Isle, ME, Penland School of Crafts, NC. He is the principal developer in the USA of the shell-structures technique and its vocabulary (1974); repeated tributes from contemporary smiths for his valuable instruction. Workshops in Lapland, Finland, 1995–96. Author of *Form Emphasis for Metalsmiths* (1978).

Charter member, SNAG; membership committee, 1970–82. Finnish Ministry of Education, Master status, 1964; League of Precious Metal Industry, Finland, Diploma for meritorious lifetime work, 1975; gold medal for professional loyalty, 1992. Fellow, American Craft Council, 1987. Excellence in Art Award, Art and Education Council, St Louis, 1996. Numerous exhibitions and commissions.[12]

Heikki Seppa was a name that I soon encountered when I first came to an interest in modern silversmithing. I turned to him at the outset of this project to request his participation. We eventually met at the Seattle SNAG conference in 1998. I have heard and read repeated expressions of pleasure and gratitude from many artists in this collection who have profited from his instruction and pioneering techniques. I was much pleased to receive a personal note from him in which he expressed his appreciation of this enterprise in support of the craft.

Cake slice

Sterling silver

St Louis, Missouri, 1992

Length 10 in. (25.5 cm)

Weight 11.8 oz (366 g)

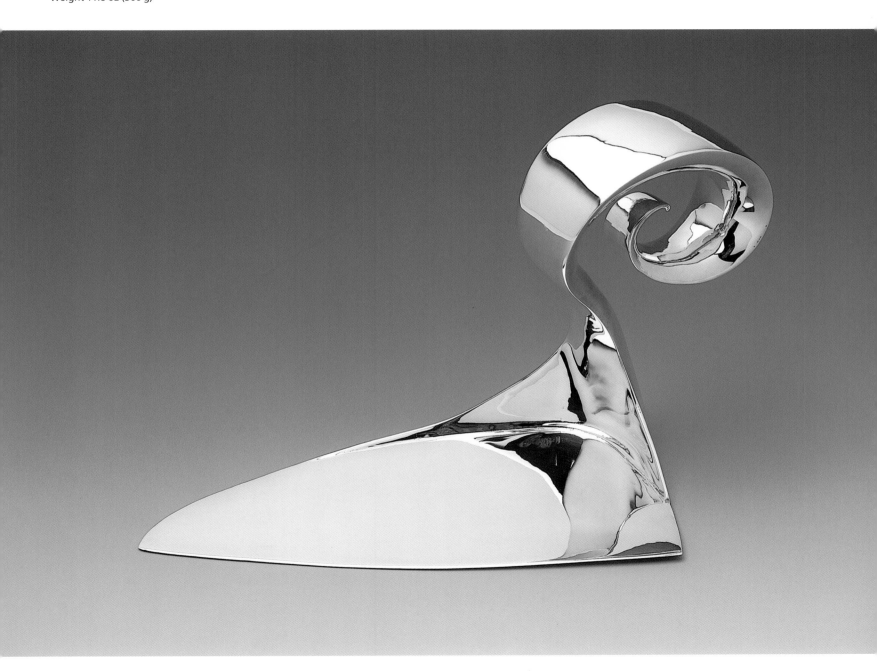

Helen Shirk

Pastry slice
Sterling silver and 14k gold
LaMesa, California, 1994
Length 12 in. (30.5 cm)
Weight 4.2 oz (132 g)

The server has a narrow triangular blade made up of several long irregular strips running most of the length of the blade and overlapped double in most places. The surface is further embellished by laid-on, irregular, narrow, gold strips. The handle is constituted of five strips, all of convex form so as to make an irregularly rounded hollow handle of roughly oval cross-section. The surface is decorated on top of the blade and both sides of the handle by a scored, engraved effect that was achieved by irregular hammer blows with a sharply scored hammer face, and which gives the surface a most attractive, scintillating, bright-cut, crystalline appearance. The server proves to be quite functional for both cake and pastry.

This server is of pronouncedly individual design: a freely formed version of the infrequent, small, mid-eighteenth-century pastry trowel of that time (see chapter 3). The style is a very personal one. It draws from the patterns and images of growth, life and death that the artist sees in nature. It is itself almost like a 'found object'; a natural specimen that holds all the surprise of a glinting rock embedded in a stratum. Shirk has exploited with boldness the huge range of textural effects that are possible in silver.

Artist's philosophy/statement: "This server was the first piece I made after my return from Australia and bears the imprint of that intense six-month experience. Photographs and drawings made during that time … reflect my compelling fascination with the shards of nature from both land and sea. Pen sketches of fragments of rock, leaves, shells and plants investigate the process by which each grow and disintegrate and examine the variant beauty that is the residue. Leaf litter on the forest floor, layered in an undisturbed and natural pattern, enveloped in quietness interrupted only by the sound of wind and birds, created the visual language seen in the Rabinovitch server. Layers of deliberately selected leaf-like forms, each a deeply textured shape in silver with surface and edges carefully hammered for subtle and infinite variation, form the body and handle of the piece. Wandering lines of textured gold weave in and out, staying the eye in certain areas of greater intricacy. Exploration of the intrinsic beauty of the reflective silver and the tranquillity of its mood were both important considerations in relation to the theme for the server."

Born: Buffalo, New York, 1942

Training and work: Skidmore College, BS, 1963, under Earl Pardon; Indiana University, MFA, 1969; study at Kunsthaandvaerkerskolen, Copenhagen, Denmark, 1963–64. Assistant professor, Indiana University, 1971–73; instructor, jewellery and metalsmithing, Des Moines Art Museum, Iowa, 1973–75; professor of art, San Diego State University, 1975– ; lecturer, Camberwell School of Arts, London, 1983; exchange professor, Curtin University, Perth, Australia, 1993.

Distinguished member, SNAG; American Craft Council. Since 1972, around a dozen awards for promise, merit, excellence and creativity at exhibitions, galleries, institutions *etc.*, including two NEA fellowships and a Fulbright grant. Well over two hundred one-person and group exhibitions at museums, galleries, universities and art centres in the USA, Australia, France, Korea, UK, Canada, Germany and Japan. Innumerable lectures, workshops, juries, summer or visiting faculty/artist in USA, UK and Australia. Citations of work or reviews in several dozen magazines and books.[13] Shirk's work is included in well over a dozen public collections of major museums and galleries in the USA and abroad, including: Smithsonian Institution, Victoria and Albert Museum, National Museum of Modern Art, Kyoto.

I first met Helen in 1990 at a gallery in her home town of San Diego at the opening of a jewellery exhibition by Flora Book (q.v.). Shortly afterwards she agreed to accept this commission. We later had the pleasure of entertaining her at our home in Seattle when she gave a workshop at the Pratt Art Center in 1991.

Nancy Slagle

Cake slice
Sterling silver
Lubbock, Texas, 1998
Length 10⅝ in. (27 cm)
Weight 8.9 oz (227 g)

The sixteen-gauge blade has a trowel shape with rounded tip and polished finish. The blade is pierced with groups of parallel slots. It turns up sharply at the rear to an arched apron, from which a unique, imaginative, three-dimensional handle rises in the form of a male figure. The figure is made as two silhouette box structures soldered to the apron but split and joined over their interiors by boxes. The top box has three rib slits and a long triangular opening that defines the legs and shows a gender indicator; this 'shadow box' has a white reticulated finish. The back box has a cusped slot to represent the buttocks of the figure. The handle has a wire-brush finish.

The symbolic importance of the number three appears to dominate the design concept of Slagle's server. It is at once uniquely distinctive and timeless, almost totemic. The triangular form of the flat blade is echoed in the three-dimensional head and shoulders of the handle. The repetition of three fretted lines on blade and handle act as a staccato emphasis. This is a powerful object, drawing on ancient messages that communicate across time, place and culture.

Artists's philosophy/statement: "This work employs function as a means of creating modern ritual. The functional object is my means of expression and a definition of form. Planes and curves, static and kinetic, hard and soft, yin and yang, all these questions of balance are evident in the resolution of form. Through the manipulations of these elements, energy and vitality become apparent. My recent forms have gradually become more sensual and volumetric: these rounded, full, pregnant shapes are achieved through die-forming as a technical means to my aesthetic goals. The server features a die-formed figure that holds and secures the softly triangular blade. The male and female reference incorporated in the server is a metaphor for the ritual aspects of dining and sharing of sustenance and social intercourse. The act of dining is a pleasurable, sensuous experience. The sharing of a meal resonates and reflects many rich aspects of life. The variety of texture, hard and soft, plain and rich, enhances the surface of the form. The textured surface supports the sensual aspects of the handle. The blade is left smooth as a functional consideration and contrasting surface."

Born: Mason City, Iowa, 1958

Training and work: Drake University, Des Moines, Iowa, BFA, metalwork and jewellery design, 1980; Indiana University, MFA, 1987. Associate professor, Texas Tech. University, Lubbock, 1997– ; assistant professor, Sul Ross State University, Alpine, Texas, 1989–90. Independent studio and commission work. Has given workshops at the Arrowmont School of Arts and Crafts, TN; at Penland School of Crafts, NC, and at the Michigan Silversmiths' Guild, Ann Arbor; and numerous lectures at institutes and universities.

Many jurors' and merit awards at exhibitions. National Endowment for the Arts grant, 1988; the Chapter Founders Award, 1986, and the Bachmura Award in Art, 1987, Indiana University. Museum Guild Purchase Award, Museum of Arts and Science, Evansville, IN, 1986; honourable mention Towle Student Sterling Design Competition, NY, 1984. Innumerable exhibitions at museums, galleries and invitational juried shows. Work in the collections of the Art Institute of Chicago, Evansville, in museums and private collections. Her work has been cited in books, journals and newspapers.[14]

I met Nancy for the first time at the SNAG conference in Seattle in 1998. Her work was well known to me from many references in the craft journals.

Fish slice

Sterling silver with gilt handle and citrine stone

Atlanta, Georgia, 1992

Length 12 ¾ in. (32.5 cm)

Weight 11.4 oz (354 g)

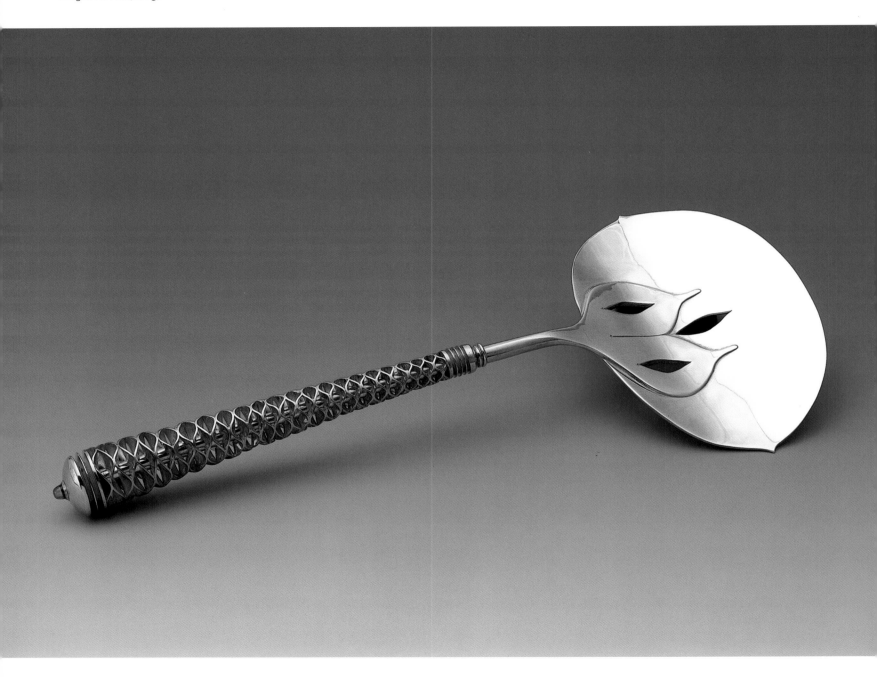

Julia Woodman

The forged blade has the transverse oval shape of the eighteenth-century Dutch fish slice, but is teased to positive cusps on each side. The handle stem is applied to a large, pierced, double-foliate junction on the top of the blade. The handle is of cannon shape made from pressed disks to produce a honeycomb tessellated structure and gilded to emphasize both the honey connection and to obviate the need for cleaning. The handle terminates in a bezel with a citrine stone that complements the gilding.

It is interesting to note that Woodman's work incorporates two eighteenth-century stylistic features not known in British fabrications of slices: the Dutch oval blade and the Scandinavian cannon handle. What appears to be an eclectic historicist approach has produced something contemporary and unique. One feels that the artist has almost subliminally absorbed past responses and selected those that work and harmonize with her own interests and skills. Perhaps this server, more than any of the others, speaks of the complexities of artistic inspiration. It illustrates a dictum of Henry Moore, who spoke of "universal shapes to which everybody is subconsciously conditioned". It reveals the timelessness of lovely shape and good design.

Artist's philosophy/statement: "My idea for a practical and elegantly simple server was inspired by a new technique, called three-dimensional tessellation. It lends itself to an overall decorative texture. The shape created by the negative space inspired both the spatula portion and the boss of this serving tool – a piece that is both useful and can stand alone as a work of art, a sculpture."

Born: Ashville, North Carolina, 1933

Training and work: Pratt Institute, New York, certificate in industrial design, 1955; Georgia State University, BFA, 1989, MFA, 1995, in metalwork with Richard Mafong. Sometime instructor at Penland School of Crafts, NC, 1993, 1995, and Spruille Center for the Arts, Atlanta, 1995–96. Workshop study with many distinguished artists, including Mary Lee Hu, Harold O'Connor, on five occasions with Heikki Seppa, and with others.

First place, Georgia State University Presidential Medallion Design; flatware winner, National Student Sterling Design Competition, 1991, 1994; second place, Georgia Arts, 1996; Penland Student Exhibition, 1996. Numerous textile and silverware commissions for churches, Georgia State University and individuals. Various exhibitions at corporations, including Tiffany and Fortunoff, galleries and museums. Her work has been the subject of a number of articles.[15]

I was first attracted to Julia's work by the elegance of her (first) prize-winning fish-server pair in the National Student Design Competition. We kept in touch throughout her Master's degree studies and finally met at the exhibition of this collection at the National Ornamental Metals Museum, Memphis, in 1996. I later visited her and her husband in Atlanta and saw some of her large commissions – metalwork and textiles – at first hand.

Kee-Ho Yuen

Fish slice
Sterling silver with stone finial
Cedar Fall, Iowa, 1995
Length 13 ¼ in. (33.5 cm)
Total weight 9.3 oz (289 g)

The blade is of elongated, pointed, trowel shape with rounded sides, reminiscent of a number of eighteenth-century Continental implements. The leading edges are waved and there is a protruding drop-shape feature on the left front edge. A polished, narrow, circumscribing band around the blade contains a brushed surface. It is decorated with an etched fish, in negative, in scrolled wave lines; a fountain of polished droplets rises towards the tip. A rear apron rises abruptly (1 ⅜ in.; 3.5 cm) at the back of the blade; it has a multi-curved chrysanthemum-like contour and an applied strengthening strap; it holds an up-sloping cannon-end handle that has a Corian ring finial, and half-round closures at both ends of the handle.

This server represents a consummate blend of eighteenth-century European form and Far Eastern style of decoration. Simplicity of form and elaborate ornamentation have also resulted in a blending of the modern and the traditional, making it a timeless object that crosses cultures. Yuen has exploited the different textures that are possible on silver through sanding, brushing and polishing to create a rich surface pattern that contrasts with the smooth simple design of the handle. His sensitivity to surface patterning can be connected to the flat-chasing of the English silversmiths Rod Kelly and Michael Lloyd (q.v.).

Artist's philosophy/statement: "When I designed this server, I chose a neutral, realistic, fish image. … I prefer a dynamic design such as the movement of the lines, water and fish. Technical handling, such as the direction of sanding and partly polished images of water and fish, contribute to the movement of the viewer's eyes over the piece, adding to the overall dynamic … of the piece. … Some people might find tension between the expected elegance of a silver fish server and its resemblance to a construction tool. However, I feel that it is a playful combination of its honest form as a tool with the fine decoration of an elegant silver server. It is refreshing to experience how these two qualities interact. What I enjoy is the totality of the piece as a single object."

Born: Hong Kong, 1956
Training and work: Chinese University of Hong Kong, BA, 1983; University of Iowa, MA, 1988; MFA, 1989 under Chunghi Choo (q.v.); work with Professor Lee Fuk Wa, CUHK, sculpture, 1982–85; teacher at Hong Kong Salesian Secondary School, 1983–86. Jewellery designer and technician with M.C. Ginsberg, Iowa City, 1986–88; University of Northern Iowa, assistant professor, 1989–94; associate professor, 1994– .

First place, National Craft Competition, Lancaster, PA, 1987; scholarships, University of Iowa, 1987–89; third place, National Student Silver Design Competition, 1989; Ariel Gallery Registry Award, New York, 1991. Summer fellowships, University of Northern Iowa, 1990, 1992. A very active decade and a half of solo and group exhibitions in museums and galleries throughout the USA and abroad in the UK, Hong Kong and Taiwan. Various private commissions.

I met Kee-Ho (Tony) at the exhibition in 1995 at Goldsmiths' Hall, where he took a leading role in promoting further contacts between British and American silversmiths. While trained by Chunghi Choo (q.v.), he has clearly developed his own style. We met again at the SNAG conference in Seattle in 1998.

6 Information

Notes

Notes to chapter 1

1 B.S. Rabinovitch, *Antique Silver Servers for the Dining Table*, Concord, MA (Joslin Hall Publishing), 1991

2 Bruce Metcalf, 'Recent Sightings', *Metalsmith*, XVII, no 3, 1997, p. 10

3 P. Cannon-Brookes, *Omar Ramsden 1873–1939: Centenary Exhibition of Silver*, exhib. cat., Birmingham Museums and Art Gallery, 1973; Tony Ford, 'The Crafts Council', *Goldsmiths' Review*, 1991–92, pp. 36–37

Notes to chapter 2

1 Vanessa Brett, 'Silver Today: The Role of the Client', *The Silver Society Journal*, no. 8, 1996, p. 514

Notes to chapter 3

1 An extended account may be found in B.S. Rabinovitch, *Antique Silver Servers for the Dining Table*, Concord, MA (Joslin Hall Publishing), 1991

Notes to chapter 4

1 W. Godfrey Allen, introduction to *British Silverwork*, exhib. cat., London, Goldsmiths' Hall, 1951

2 Victoria Geibel, 'Silver Expression', *Metalsmith*, X, no. 4, 1990, p. 61, quoting Richard Mawdsley

3 Eric Turner, 'Modernism and English Silver', in *Victoria and Albert Museum Album*, London (Victoria and Albert Museum) 1987, p. 222

4 Veronika Schwarzinger, 'Silver: A Valuable, a Utensil, a Work of Art, a Material in Dialogue', in *Contemporary European Silverwork*, Munich 1993, p. 20

5 B.S. Rabinovitch and H. Clifford, 'Slices of Silver', *American Craft*, LVII, no. 4, 1997, p. 54

6 George Ravensworth Hughes, *The Worshipful Company of Goldsmiths as Patrons of their Craft, 1919–1953*, London (Goldsmiths' Company) 1964

7 *Modern Silver*, London (Goldsmiths' Company) 1954

8 Robert Welch, *Hand and Machine*, Chipping Campden (Robert Welch) 1986, p.17

9 Toni Greenbaum, 'The College in Context', in Greenbaum (ed.), *Lifetime Achievements*, Memphis, TN (National Ornamental Metals Museum), 1993, p. 6

10 Lisa Hamel, 'Metalwork in the 20th Century', *Metalsmith*, XIV, no. 4, 1994, p. 29

11 *Ibid.*, p. 60

12 Rod Kelly, 'Rod Kelly, Silversmith', *The Silver Society Journal,* no. 4, 1993, p. 144

13 Marina Vaizey, 'The Crafts Renaissance', *The Antique Collector*, LXIV, no.1, 1992/93, p. 42

14 Eric Turner, 'Post-War Silver', in Charles Truman (ed.), *Sotheby's Concise Encyclopedia of Silver*, London (Conran Octopus) 1993, p. 177

15 Greenbaum, quoting Eidelberg, in M. Eidelberg (ed.), *Design 1935–1965: What Modern Was*, New York (Harry Abrams) 1991, p. 51

16 Marina Vaizey, *Shining Through*, exhib. cat., London, Crafts Council Gallery, 1995, p. 7

17 David McOwan, 'Silversmithing in Australia', in David McOwan (ed.), *Contemporary Australian Hollow-Ware*, exhib. cat., Australia, City of Hamilton Art Gallery, 1991, p. 4

18 Eric Turner, 'Modernism and English Silver', in *Victoria and Albert Museum Album*, 1984, p. 241

19 John Culme, *Nineteenth-Century Silver,* London (Country Life) 1977, p. 222

20 P. Cannon-Brookes, *Omar Ramsden 1873–1939: Centenary Exhibition of Silver*, exhib. cat., Birmingham Museums and Art Gallery, 1973, p. 8

21 *British Silverwork* 1951, p. 11

22 Philippa Glanville, *Silver in England,* London (Allen & Unwin) 1987, p. 141

23 John Lang, *Lichfield Cathedral Silver Commission*, Lichfield (The Dean and Chapter of Lichfield Cathedral) 1991, p. 40

24 Annelies Krekel-Aalberse, *Art Nouveau and Art Deco Silver*, London (Thames and Hudson) 1989, p. 68

25 Nancy Troy, *Modernism and the Decorative Arts in France*, New Haven and London (Yale University Press) 1991

26 Michael Rowe, 'Inheriting Modernism', in H. Clifford (ed.), *Twentieth Century Silver*, London, Crafts Council Gallery, 1993, p. 35

27 *Designed for Delight: Alternative Aspects of Twentieth Century Decorative Arts*, *exhib.* flyer, Montreal Museum of Decorative Arts Exhibition, 1997

28 Deyan Sudjic, 'Sottsass and Co.', *Crafts*, no. 59, November/December 1982

29 Barbara Radice, *Memphis Research: Experiences, Results, Failures and Successes of New Design*, London (Memphis) 1983, p. 62

30 Christiane Weber-Stöber, 'The European Situation in Silversmith Art', in *Contemporary Silverwork*, London 1983

31 Hamel 1994, p. 29

32 Roseanne Raab, 'Silver: An American Tradition', in C. Weber (ed.), *Silbergestaltung*, Munich (Klinkhardt & Biermann) 1992, p. 63

33 Gerhard Dietrich, 'Autonomous Form – Absolute Function', in *The Eloquent Vessel*, ed. Werner Bünck, Cologne (Museum für Angewandte Kunst) 1992, p. 5

34 Michael Hall, 'Ring Leaders', *Country Life*, 26 September 1996, pp. 84–85

35 Robert S. Silver, '20th-Century Silver', *What's On*, 13 October 1993, p. 24

36 For example, *Royal Goldsmiths, Garrard Design and Patronage in the Twentieth Century*, London 1993; *Silver to Dine For!*, exhib. cat., London, Leighton House, 1996; *Living Silver*, Asprey, London 1997

37 For example, *Contemporary European Silverware*, London 1993; *A Sparkling Party*, Antwerp 1995

38 Martha Sung-Won Lee, 'The Current Development in Hollow and Flatware Design at the Korean Universities' in C. Weber (ed.), *Silbergestaltung,* Munich (Klinkhardt & Biermann) 1992, p. 130

39 *Ibid.*, p. 75

40 Simone ten Hompel, interviewed on *Woman's Hour*, BBC Radio 4, London, December 1996

Notes to chapter 5

1 Helen Clifford, 'Unity in Variety: Strength in Diversity. Cutlery, Craft and Culture and the Association of British Designer-Silversmiths', in *Millennium Canteen*, exhib. cat., Sheffield City Museum and Art Gallery, 1998, pp. 9 ff.

Notes to chapter 6
British Silversmiths

1 *Brian Asquith, Silversmith,* exhib. cat., London, Goldsmiths' Hall, 1992; Jeremy Myerson, 'Sources of Inspiration', *Crafts*, September/October 1993, p. 44; David Beasley, 'Silver Initiatives', *Goldsmiths' Review*, 1996

2 Christopher Levy, 'Man of Metal', *Sotheby's Preview*, May/June 1990, p. 23

3 *Lichfield Cathedral Silver Commission* 1991; Chris Walton, *British Goldsmiths of Today,* exhib. cat., London Goldsmiths' Hall, 1992; Chris Walton, *British Master Goldsmiths*, exhib. cat., London, Goldsmiths' Hall, 1997

4 Michael Hall, 'Taking a shine to silver', *The Times*, London, 5 March 1994

5 R. Edgecumbe and J. Stancliffe, *Kevin Coates*, exhib. cat., London, Victoria and Albert Museum, 1985, p. 5

6 Compare *British Goldsmiths of Today* 1992

7 V. Becher, *Harpers & Queen*, October 1993

8 *Kevin Coates* 1985, p. 6

9 *Kevin Coates: One-Man Show*, exhib. cat., London, Goldsmiths' Hall, 1991, p. 12

10 *Leslie Durbin: Fifty Years of Silversmithing,* exhib. cat., London, Goldsmiths' Hall, 1982, p. 23

11 G.W. Rawlins, 'Silver by Leslie Durbin', *International Nickel Magazine*, no. 1, 1968, p. 42

12 *Craftsman Inspired by Minerva*, London (Raithby, Lawrence and Co.) 1968, p. 4

13 C. Walton, 'A Man of Many Faces', *Goldsmiths' Gazette*, April 1986, p. 24

14 Adapted from Amanda Fielding, 'Silver Launch Liberty Ltd', *Craft Notes*, 1993, p. 61

15 Simone ten Hompel, interviewed on *Woman's Hour,* BBC Radio 4, London, December 1996

16 Adapted from Amanda Game and Hans Stofer, *Beyond the Line*, exhib. cat., Edinburgh, The Scottish Gallery, 1995, p. 3

17 *Contemporary Silver Tableware*, exhib. cat., London, Goldsmiths' Hall, 1996, p. 15

18 Rod Kelly, 'Rod Kelly, Silversmith', *The Silver Society Journal*, no. 4, 1993, p. 139

19 *Lichfield Cathedral Silver Commission* 1991, p. 42

20 Adapted from *Rising Stars*, exhib. cat., London, Goldsmiths' Hall, 1990, p. 13; see also note 18

21 Helen Clifford, 'Contemporary Silverware 1995', *Crafts*, no. 135, July/August 1995, p. 57; Margot Coatts, 'The Living Silver Collection', *Crafts*, no. 140, May/June 1996, p. 55

22 *Ibid.*

23 Clare Beck, Crafts Council Shop leaflet, London (Victoria and Albert Museum) 1994

24 *Lichfield Cathedral Silver Commission* 1991, p. 40

25 David Beasley, 'Silver for Service', *Goldsmiths' Review*, 1993/94, pp. 20–25

26 E. Lucie-Smith, *The World of the Makers*, London (Paddington Press) 1995, p. 59; J. Dormer and R. Turner, *The New Jewellery*, London (Thames and Hudson) 1985, p. 13; *British Goldsmiths of Today* 1992, p. 46

27 Quoted in *The Art of Enamelling: A Display of the Enameller's Craft*, exhib. cat., London, Goldsmiths' Hall, 1995, p. 1

28 *Lichfield Cathedral Silver Commission* 1991, p. 20

American Silversmiths

1 Sue Amendolara, 'Portfolio: Sue Amendolara', *American Craft*, LII, no. 5, 1992, p. 54; M. Hollern, 'Sue Amendolara: A Study of Nature', *Metalsmith*, XIV, no. 2, 1994, p. 43

2 L.D. Raiteri, 'Phillip Baldwin, Bladesmith', *Metalsmith*, VIII, no. 4, 1988, p. 50; M. Kangas, 'Phillip Baldwin. Forged Alliances', *Metalsmith*, XIII, no. 2, 1988, p. 30; B.J. Miller, 'The Double Edged Blade', *American Craft*, LVII, no. 1,1997, p. 68

3 C.L.E. Benesh, 'Flora Book: The Creative Spirit', *Ornament*, XVII, no. 3, 1994, p. 46; D. Standish, 'Documents Northwest', *Metalsmith*, XIII, no. 4, 1993, p. 46

4 Robert A. Rorex, 'The Energy Qi', *Metalsmith*, XI, no. 1, 1991, p. 26

5 'Cynthia Eid', *Metalsmith*, front cover, XVI, no. 3, 1996

6 M. Hamilton, 'Susan Ewing', *Metalsmith*, VIII, no. 4, 1988, p. 32; J.W. Linn, 'Susan Ewing', *American Craft*, LVI, no. 6, 1996/97, p. 38

7 'Portfolio: Robert Farrell', *American Craft*, LII, no. 4, 1992, p. 67

8 B. Penn, 'Val Link & Graduates', *Metalsmith*, XII, no. 1, 1992, p. 42

9 C.E. Licka, 'The Work of John Marshall', *American Craft*, XXXXV, no. 2, April/May 1985, p. 10; C. Christofides, *John Marshall, Metalsmith: Selected Works 1979–1991*, exhib. cat., Memphis, TN, National Ornamental Metals Museum, 1991

10 Y.K. Okim, 'Kum-Boo: 24k Overlay on Silver', *Metalsmith*, XII, no. 2, 1992, p. 28

11 A. Fisch, 'Ronald Hayes Pearson: American Classic', *American Craft*, LII, no. 3, 1992, p. 30

12 S.H. Hamlet, 'Heikki Seppa: Form Emphasis', *Metalsmith*, VI, no. 3, 1986, p. 57

13 J. Keaffaher, 'Helen Shirk', *Metalsmith*, X, no. 4, 1990, p. 15; B. Douglas, 'Helen Shirk', *Metalsmith*, V, no. 2, 1985, p. 43; 'Helen Shirk', *Metalsmith*, XIV, 1994, pp. 5, 21

14 R.L. Cardinale, 'National Metals Competition', *Metalsmith*, XII, 1992, p. 16; K. Bova, '1990 Metals International Exhibition', *Metalsmith*, XI, 1991, p. 46; D. and S. LaPlantz, *Jewelry/Metalwork Survey*, III, 1993, p. 208; Bob Mitchell, *1995 Metal Arts Source Book*, CD-ROM, Tampa, FL (Delta Tech)

15 A.C. Tom, 'National Student Sterling Design Competition', *Metalsmith*, XII, no. 1, 1992

Glossary

ACID ETCHING
See Etching.

ALLOY
The material formed by combining (mixing) two or more substances, of which at least one is a metal; in the present case silver and/or gold. See Silver.

ANODIZED
Oxidization process that occurs at the anode of an electrolysis cell.

ANTICLASTIC
A geometric form whose shape has the contour of the inner surface of a doughnut hole, *i.e.* which turns down in the forward (long) direction and turns up in the transverse (short) direction; cf. the shape of a mountain pass.

APRON
The turned-up rear edge of a broad blade.

ASSAY
The testing of silver items to check that the alloy or quality of metal meets legal requirements. The UK has assay offices in London, Birmingham, Sheffield and Edinburgh. See also Silver and Marks.

BASSE TAILLE
The covering of an engraved or chased metal surface with a semi-transparent enamel that reveals the underlying design and whose varied depth displays nuances of colour.

BOSS, BOLSTER
The attachment of the handle to the blade via some feature such as a V-shape, a shell *etc*. The boss (bolster) may be completely absent, as when there is a continuous one-piece transition from blade to handle, or when the handle simply descends on the blade with no accompanying structure other than the solder joint itself.

BRITANNIA
See Marks.

BURNISHING
Smoothing and polishing a surface by pressure with a hardened, rounded, polished, steel tool.

BUTLER FINISH
A popular, light-matte, surface appearance that eliminates glare and otherwise evident light scratches.

CASTING
Creating an object or parts of an object by pouring molten metal into a mould. Various techniques have been used at different times.

CHASING
Method of decorating the surface of an object from the front using punches or chasing tools of variable shapes. The technique can be used alone, or together with embossing and *repoussé*. The technique is also used to refine and define cast details, and does not entail the removal of any metal.

CLOISONNÉ; CLOISONS
A type of enamelling wherein a surface is patterned into areas divided by narrow partitions or cloisons and the spaces so created are filled with enamel(s).

CORIAN
A synthetic stoneware.

CUT-CARD
Applied decoration cut from thin sheets of silver.

DELRIN
A polyacetal plastic.

DIE FORMING
See Power stamping.

ELECTROFORMING
Method of creating an object (or copying an old one) by depositing a thin layer of metal on to a model by means of electrolysis.

EMBOSSING/*REPOUSSÉ*
Decorating silver in relief by hammering from the reverse or inside. No silver is removed. The resulting raised patterns or protuberances (bosses) are usually finished from the front, *i.e.* pushed back, by chasing (*repoussé*). See also Chasing.

ENAMELLING
Translucent glass substance used to decorate metalwork. The various methods used include *basse taille*, *champlevé*, *cloisonné* and *plique-à-jour*.

ENGRAVING
Decorating the surface of metal by cutting into it with a graver or burin and removing silver (or other material) in the desired pattern.

ETCHING
Decoration on the surface of metal using acid or other chemicals to remove metal. The result can look similar to engraving.

FINISH
Different surface textures and colours can be given to an object by polishing using a variety of brushes, cloths and powders. The following finishes are mentioned in the catalogue: bright, brushed, satin, burnished, bright butler, butler, mirror, pickle, scratch brushed, sharp brushed, white.

FLATWARE
Term used today synonymously with cutlery, to describe spoons, forks, knives and other tableware, that are, nominally, two-dimensional.

FORGED
Metal stretched or shaped by blows from a hammer with attendant changes in thickness.

GAUGE (of sheet silver)
Silversmiths acquire their raw materials from bullion dealers, specifying the gauge and size of the sheet from which they then make the object. Gauges used for this project mentioned in the text range between ten (2.6 mm) and twenty-four (0.5 mm) in (American) Brown and Sharpe measure and (roughly) twelve and twenty-five gauge in (British) Birmingham measure.

GOLD
Precious metal. Standards that are legally saleable vary from country to country. Hallmarking regulations in the UK changed in January 1999: 22 carat (k), 18k, 14k and 9k are accepted.

GRANULATION
Decoration of small particles of gold or silver that is applied to the surface of an object by first copper plating and then heating to 'solder' (sinter) the pieces together.

HOLLOW-WARE
Articles such as drinking, pouring and serving vessels (jugs, tankards, mugs, goblets, bowls) that are three-dimensional; cf. flatware.

HYDRAULIC PRESS
See Power stamping.

JAPANESE METALWORK
Including *mokumé gané* (multi-layered metal combinations); *shakudo* (alloy of gold and copper, with a little silver, principally purple or black in colour); *shibuichi* (alloy of silver and copper, with a little gold, dull silver-grey).

KUM-BOO
Application of gold foil to a surface by burnishing.

LASER
A device for putting out a sharply defined beam of (coherent) light.

MARKS
The UK has a long history of regulation (in England since 1300). Hallmarking regulations in the UK changed in January 1999. Previously, two standards were permitted: Britannia (950 parts of silver per thousand) and sterling (925 parts of silver per thousand). With the new system, standards of 800 and 999 can be sold, but are subject to new marking regulations. In the USA, sterling is the accepted standard, but no formal assay regulation of quality exists, as in the UK.

MOKUMÉ GANÉ (wood grain)
See Japanese metalwork.

NAVETTE
Boat-shaped; as for an ellipse drawn to a point at each end.

NICKEL SILVER
Alloy of copper, nickel and zinc, sometimes also called Nevada silver or, in the nineteenth century, German silver. Chinese *paktong* is an early variant. Contains no silver; the composition is variable.

OXIDIZED
Method of colouring silver chemically.

PALLADIUM
Metallic element resembling platinum.

PATINATION
The formation of a surface skin or coloration on a metal.

PEENED
The texture created by striking the metal with a sharp rectangular-faced hammer.

PLANISHED
The smoothing of the surface of the metal by delicate blows from a light flat-faced hammer.

PLATE, PLATED
The term 'plate' – not the dish! – refers to silver objects; compare the Spanish word *plata* (silver). It is not to be confused with the word plated, which refers to a base-metal object that has been covered with a thin layer of silver or gold (or other metal) by electrodeposition (electroplate) or other means (Sheffield plate; close plate).

POWER STAMPING
Process of shaping or moving metal by application of pressure; also die forming.

PRESSURE (HYDRAULIC) FORMING
See Power stamping.

RAISING
The process of shaping a sheet of metal by hammering and without changing thickness.

REPOUSSÉ
See embossing.

SHAKUDO
See Japanese metalwork.

SHEET
See Gauge.

SHELLFORM; SHELL STRUCTURE
Combination of clastic forms; see Anticlastic and Synclastic.

SHIBUICHI
See Japanese metalwork.

SILVER
Pure silver is used in electroplating but is too soft to be durable alone. It is alloyed with other metals, usually copper, with small additions, sometimes, of other metals for specific applications and alloy properties. See also Marks.

SOLDERED
Joining of two pieces of metal by use of a lower-melting intermediate.

SPINNING
Method of forming an object by using a lathe and forcing a disk of silver to conform to a wooden or steel form.

STERLING
See Silver.

SYNCLASTIC
A geometric form that has the contour of the outside surface of a doughnut, *i.e.* one that turns down in both the forward (long) direction and transverse (short) direction; cf. the surface shape of an American football.

WEIGHTS
Troy ounces are used. 1 troy ounce = 20 pennyweights (dwt); 1 oz = 31.1 g.

Further Reading

In addition to the articles and exhibition catalogues listed in the preceding notes, the following may be of interest:

Books

Esbjørn Hiort, *Modern Danish Silver*, London (New York Museum Books) 1954

Graham Hughes, *Modern Silver Throughout the World 1880–1967*, New York 1967

Gillian Naylor, *The Arts and Crafts Movement*, London (Studio Vista) 1971

Fiona McCarthy, *British Design Since 1880*, London 1982

Christopher Frayling, *The Royal College of Art: One Hundred and Fifty Years of Art and Design,* London (Barrie and Jenkins) 1987

Joost Willink (ed.), *Silver of a New Era: International Highlights of Precious Metalwork 1880–1940*, Rotterdam (Museum Boymans van Beuningen) 1992

Irena Goldscheider and Alena Zapletalová, *Metalmorphosis: Tradition and Innovation in British Silver and Metalwork 1880–1998,* exhib. cat., Prague, Museum of Decorative Arts, 1998, esp. pp. 49–55: I. Goldscheider, 'Silversmithing and Metalwork Courses at Art Colleges in Britain'

Anna Maria Dryden, 'Commercial Silversmiths and the British Silver Trade during the Inter-War Years', *Decorative Arts Journal*, no.17

Magazines and Journals

Metalsmith (USA)
Ornament (USA)
Silver Magazine (USA)
Crafts (UK)
The Silver Society Journal, annual publication [22 Orlando Road, London SW4 OLF]
Goldsmiths' Review, annual publication [The Worshipful Company of Goldsmiths, Foster Lane, London EC2V 6BN]

Useful Addresses

United Kingdom

Worshipful Company of Goldsmiths
Goldsmiths' Hall
Foster Lane
London EC2V 6BN

Association of British Designer Silversmiths (ABDS)
9 The Leathermarket
Weston Street
London SE1 3ER

Crafts Council
44a Pentonville Road
London N1 9BY

Society of Designer Craftsmen
24 Rivington Street
London EC2A 3DU

British Society of Enamellers
30 Kensington Square
London W8 5ES

British Art Medal Society
Department of Coins and Medals
British Museum
London WC1B 3DS

Contemporary Applied Arts
2 Percy Street
London W1P 9FA

P&O Makower Trust
Bishopsland
Dunsden
Oxfordshire RG4 9NR

School of Silversmithing, Metalsmithing and Jewellery
Royal College of Art
Kensington Gore
London SW7 2EV

United States of America

Society of North American Goldsmiths (SNAG)
2275 Amigo Drive
Missoula
MT 59808

American Craft Council
72 Spring Street
New York
NY 10012

Society of American Silversmiths (SAS)
PO Box 704
Chepachet
RI 02814–0704

National Ornamental Metals Museum
374 Metal Museum Drive
Memphis
TN 38106

In addition, the biographical notes in the texts on the silversmiths (chapter 6) and the notes on the various chapters (pp. 154–55) contain the names of numerous colleges and of many awards and regular exhibitions, which may be of use.

The magazines listed on this page have copious information about smiths, exhibitions, schools, conferences, and many other special features. The Society of American Silversmiths is pleased to offer assistance and advice on commissioning silver. The Crafts Council, London, also offers help and listings.

Where to see or buy metal and other craftwork

Many (most) museums in the larger cities of the USA and UK have displays of metalwork, antique and/or contemporary, and retail shops. The same is true of many two- and four-year colleges and universities. Private/commercial art and craft galleries may be found throughout both nations.

Colleges offering silversmithing courses

The Membership Directory of SNAG (see above) has a comprehensive listing of US schools, colleges and institutes that give courses in metalsmithing and jewellery work.

In the UK there has been considerable reorganization of courses, colleges and universities in recent years. Many of the colleges and awards listed in the silversmiths' biographies have changed their title several times in the last decade, which can cause confusion. For the purpose of the listings in the preceding pages, titles have been simplified and given some consistency, though this may have resulted in the exact title being inaccurate for the dates given. The present (1999) titles for those most frequently quoted are as follows:

Royal College of Art, London

Sir John Cass Department of Art, London Guildhall University

The London Institute, Camberwell College of Arts

Central St Martin's College of Art and Design

School of Design, University of Brighton

School of Jewellery and Silversmithing, The University of Central England, Birmingham

School of Silversmithing, Goldsmithing and Jewellery Design, Kent Institute of Art and Design, Fort Pitt, Rochester, Kent

Gray's School of Art at The Robert Gordon University, Aberdeen

Duncan of Jordanstone College of Art and Design, Dundee

University of Ulster, Belfast

Index

Colleges, awards, exhibitions *etc.* mentioned in the biographical information of silversmiths have not been indexed; however, some of the major commissions quoted have been included. Figures in bold refer to the detailed entries in Chapter 6: The Collection.

ABDS, see Association of British Designer Silversmiths
Aberdeen Museum and Art Gallery 52
Amendolara, Suzanne 20, 27, **96–97**
America's Cup trophy 140
American Craft Museum, NY 98, 118
Appleby, Malcolm 24, 27, **28–29**, 40, 76, 77, 88
Architects' Company 76
Armouries, Royal 28
Ascot, Diamond Stakes and trophies 43, 75, 80, 86, 105
Ashbee, C.R. 20
Asprey & Garrard [and Asprey] 11, 18
Asquith, Brian 10, 27, **30–31**
Association of British Designer Silversmiths [ABDS] 18, 62, 95, 158
Ayrton Metals 75

BBC 88
Bailey, Banks and Biddle fig. 8
Baker, Martin 24, 27, **32–33**
Baldwin, Phillip 23, 24, 27, **98–99**
Barishnikov, Mikhail 124
Bassant, Norma 80
Bauhaus 19, 21, 55
Baxendale, Ralph G. 18, 65
Beardslee, Candace 27, **100–01**, 114
Belvoir, Paul 80
Benney, Gerald 18, 27, **34–35**, 58. 65
Birch, Derick 65
Birmingham Museums and Art Gallery 40, 48
Blunt & Wray 46
Book, Flora 27, **102–03**, 114, 146
Boston, Museum of Fine Arts 102, 106, 140
Bristol Museum and Art Gallery 52
British Art Medal Society 36, 91

Brogden, Alex 24, 27, **36–37**, 137
Brophy, Michael 11, 24, 27, **104–05**
Bulgari 11
Butler, Robert 24, 27, 33, **106–07**

Callender, Wade 23, 24, 27, **108–09**
Calvert, Ian 80
Cambridge, Corpus Christi College 36
Cambridge, Lucy Cavendish College 80
Cambridge, St John's College 56, 65, 105
Cartier 11
Chesapeake, Christ Church 105
Chicago, Art Institute of 110, 120, 148
Choo, Chunghi 27, **110–11**, 134, 152
Christofle 11
Clements, Eric 18
Coates, Kevin 21, 24, 27, **38–39**
Coeur d'Alene Mines Corporation 143
Cogswell, John 16, 27, **112–13**
Colorado, University of 105
Commonwealth Games 73
Comyns, William Ltd 46
Conway, Ros 24, 27, **40–41**
Cooper-Hewitt Museum 75
Cortland County Arts Council, NY 113
Courts, David 27, **42–43**
Crafts Council, London 18, 31, 36, 40, 51, 62, 65, 67, 75, 79, 80, 83, 84, 91, 158
Craver, Margaret 19
Curriers' Company 76

Daniel, Thomas fig. 4
De Beers 33, 43, 75, 105
Denn, Basile fig. 3
Devlin, Stuart 73
Disney, Walt 33
Dobson, Frank 31
Downing Street, see Silver Trust, The
Doyle, Roger 88
Dresser, Christopher 20
Dublin Castle 68
Dubois, Gottfried fig. 10
Durbin, Leslie 18, 20, 27, **44–45**, 73

East Anglia, University of 76
Eastern Washington University 124
Eaton, Elizabeth fig. 6
Edinburgh, Old Kirk 73
Eid, Cynthia 19, 27, 101, **114–15**
Eidelberg, Martin 20
Elson, Anthony 27, **46–47**
Ewing, Susan 27, **116–17**

Farrell, Robert 20, 27, 56, **118–19**
Fisher, Alexander 84
Fitzwilliam Museum, Cambridge 18, 65
Fortunoff 23, 143, 151
Fowler, Charles 43
Frederick, William 12, 20, 24, 27, **120–21**

Gackenbach, David 27, **122–23**
Garrard 11, 33, 44, 51
Gaynard, Skip 27, **124–25**
Gebelein silversmiths 106
Georgia State University 151
Gilbert, Walter [Wally] 12, 15, 27, **48–49**
Glasgow Museum 52
Goldsmiths, Worshipful Company of 9, 10, 18, 28, 31, 33, 34, 36, 39, 40, 43, 44, 46, 48, 51, 52, 55, 56, 58, 62, 65, 67, 73, 75, 76, 79, 80, 83, 84, 88, 91, 95, 105, 158
Good, Michael 109
Goodden, Robert 18, 34, 65
Gorham 11, 12, 15, 105
Grant, Norman 88
Guild of Handicraft 20

Hackett, Bill 27, **42–43**
Hamel, Lisa 22
Harris, Gareth 27, 56, **86–87**
Harvard University 105, 120, 137
Heer, Bernard Wilhelm fig. 12
Hill, Reginald 18
Hofken, Jan van't fig. 9
Hompel, Simone ten 19, 23, 24, 27, **50–51**, 55
Hope, Adrian 24, 27, **52–53**

East Anglia, University of 76
Horner, Roger 27, **126–27**
Hu, Mary Lee 102, 151
Huntley, Justine 10, 27, **54–55**
Hussein, King of Jordan 33
Hutton 12

Inchbald School of Design 36
Indianapolis 500 105
International Silver 11, 12
Iran, Shah of 73
Ironmongers' Company 76
Ivanovic, Kay 27, **56–57**

Jensen, Georg 21, 144
Jewish Museum, NY 113, 132
John Paul II, Pope 124
Jones, Sarah 106

Kelly, Rod 12, 19, 20, 24, 27, **58–61**, 152
Knight, Chris 22, 24, 27, **62–63**
Knox, Archibald 20
Kohler Arts Center 113
Koppel, Henning 21
Kyoto, Museum of Modern Art 146

Lambeth Palace 84
Larsen, Jack Lenor 23
Le Sage, John Hugh fig. 1
Lee, Martha Sung-Won 23
Leeds Art Galleries 67
Leeds Castle 39
Leeds City Museum 40
Lewin, Linda 52
Liberty 20, 33, 51
Lichfield Cathedral Collection 11, 31, 34, 36, 39, 58, 65, 84
Lincolnshire Museum 65
Link, Val 19, 27, 109, **128–29**
Liverpool Cathedral 46
Lloyd's Insurance 65
Lloyd, Michael 12, 20, 24, **64–65**, 152
Lotter, Matthias fig. 11
Loyen, Frances 73

MacDonald, Grant 105
Manchester Metropolitan University 70, 79
Marshall, John 13, 24, 27, 79, 83, 102, 124, **130–31**
Matzdorf, Kurt 19, 27, 113, **132–33**
McCallum, Alistair 24, 27, **66–67**
McCrory, Michael 27, **68–69**
McFadyen, Angus 24, 27, **70–71**
Mellor, David 18
Memphis 22
Mercantile Credit 80
Metropolitan Museum of Art, NY 110
Middle Temple, Hon Society of 36
Miller, Hector 27, 44, **72–73**
Mina, Jacqueline 27, **74–75**
Minnesota Museum of Art 120, 132, 137
Morris, William 20
Moss, Leonard 44
MTV 43
Murray, Michael 106
Museé des Arts Decoratifs 110
Musgrove, Peter 27, 28, **76–77**, 113

National Museum of Scotland 84
Nayler Brothers 79
Nepal, King of 46
New York State Museum 132
New York, State University of 79, 113, 132
Norwich Cathedral 76

O'Neill, Shannon 27, **78–79**
Okim, Komelia Hongja 27, **134–35**
Oneida 11, 12
Oppenheimer 86
Osman, Louis 48, 76
Ottewill, Steven 27, **80–81**

P&O Makower Trust 27, **78–79**
Padgett & Braham Ltd 86
Paisley University 88
Pearson, Ronald 24, 27, **136–37**
Peterson, David 27, **138–39**
PGA trophy 105

Portland School of Art 140
Prince of Wales, HRH The 28, 33, 34, 39
Pruden, Dunstan 34, 46
Puiforcat, Jean Emile 20

Queen, HM The 33, 34, 44

Raab, Roseanne 22, 138
Radice, Barbara 22
Ramsden, Omar 9, 20, 44
Renwick Gallery, Washington 102, 120
Rhode Island School of Design 140
Richardson, Justin 15, 24, 27, **80–81**
Rogers 12
Rowe, Michael 21
Royal College of Art 18, 19, 28
Royal Mint 91
Royal Scottish Museum 52, 65, 75, 88
Royal Society, The 28, 44, 65
Royal Yacht Squadron 73
Russell, Toby 13, 27, **82–83**, 137

St Albans Church, Wirral 79
St Peter's, Rome 140
San Lorenzo workshop 20
Schremmer, Harold 11, 27, **140–41**
Schwarzinger, Veronika 18
Schweitzer, Andrea 27, 102, **142–43**
Scottish Assembly 65
Scottish Craft Collection 52
Seppa, Heikki 21, 23, 27, 109, 128, **144–45**, 151
Shakespeare Globe Trust 91
Shiner, Cyril 18
Shipley Art Gallery 36
Shirk, Helen 20, 27, **146–47**
Short, Jane 24, 27, **84–85**
Silver Trust 10 Downing Street Collection, The 11, 28, 31, 36, 39, 56, 58, 65, 73, 79, 86
Slagle, Nancy 27, **148–49**
Smith, Dennis 27, **86–87**
Smithsonian Institution 137, 146
SNAG, see Society of North American Goldsmiths

Society of American Silversmiths 18, 113, 158
Society of North American Goldsmiths [SNAG] 18, 97, 101, 110, 113, 123, 128, 130, 132, 134, 137, 138, 144, 146, 148, 152, 158
Solberg, Ramona 102
Sottsass, Ettore Jr 22
Stalingrad sword 44
Stapley, J.E. 18
State Department, US 105
Stewart, Graham 18, 24, 27, **88–89**
Stirling University 88
Stock Exchange, London 46
Styles, Alex 18

Taylor, Joseph fig. 5
Taylor, Lucian 20, 27, **90–91**
Tiffany 11, 15, 18, 33, 105, 109, 151
Towle 12, 148
Townsend, Charles fig. 2
Triennale award, Milan 22, 31
Turner, Eric 18

Ulster, University of 68

Vaizey, Marina 20, 22
Vander, C.J. Ltd 12, 76
Venturi, Robert 105
Verlegh, R.A fig. 13
Victoria and Albert Museum 33, 39, 40, 43, 48, 51, 65, 67, 75, 79, 84, 110, 146
Vintners' Company 73

Ward, Alfred 24, 27, **92–93**
Watt, James fig. 7
Wax Chandlers' Company 76
Welch, Robert 18
Western Australia, Art Gallery of 67
White House 11, 97, 117
Whitelaw, Julie 27, **94–95**, 113
Woodman, Julia 24, 27, **150–51**

Yuen, Kee-Ho 27, **152–53**